亞洲相冊

Asia Album

《亞洲相冊》編委會

主　　　編　　汪金福

副　主　編　　張崇防、李　凱

執 行 主 編　　張　寧、查文曄、陳　健

編 委 會 成 員　曲俊雅、葉在琪、高　路、易　凌、吳　夏、湯沛沛、馮啟迪、

　　　　　　　　高　陽、劉雲非、陸曉平、姜　珊

前　言

在亞太廣袤的大地上，100 多位新華社記者每日堅守在崗位上，用鏡頭與筆墨記錄著朝陽和雨露，汗水與笑容，苦難與希望……

有時候，瞬間即是永恆。我們多彩的"日誌"，展示了一個開放包容、創新增長、互聯互通、合作共贏的亞太命運共同體，正在由理念變為行動，從願景化為現實，呈現勃勃生機，結出纍纍碩果。

我們為大家講述的故事，是亞洲故事、亞太故事，是中國與亞太的故事，也是亞太命運共同體的故事。故事的主旋律是以中國式現代化引領共同發展之路，帶動亞太國家的現代化進程，朝向構建人類命運共同體的目標攜手前進。

宏大的敘事，有時不妨以寧靜的方式宣講。沉默的照片，也能在人心裏奏響動聽的音樂。

我們希望，讀者翻開這本《亞洲相冊》，如同行走在亞細亞壯美的河山與多姿的城市之間，時而感到震撼，時而感到心動，時而發出會心的一笑。

影像不變的主角是人。從這本相冊中，我們可以看到：亞洲人民日復一日辛勤地勞作在田間與工廠，養育著全球超過一半的人口；灑紅節、潑水節、開齋節，人們在多彩的節慶日子裏歡歌高蹈；中老鐵路開通，雅萬高鐵投入運營……在這些重要歷史時刻，人們的臉上寫著光榮與夢想。合作共贏是發展的必由之路，亞洲人民共同推動經濟發展的車輪，守護共同的家園，在綠色發展的道路上不斷前行。

還能看到，阿富汗地震、湯加海嘯，當自然災害肆虐時，亞洲人民總是守望相助。

十年來，中國與"一帶一路"共建國家打造了一個個國家地標與民生工程，收穫了實打實、沉甸甸的成果。機場、港口、公路、高鐵、輕軌、電站和工業園等眾多"一帶一路"標誌性項目，向我們展示以互聯互通為主線的"發展帶"和惠及各國人民的"幸福路"。

在亞太地區，世界文化和非物質文化遺產相當豐富，其中不少是聯合國教科文組織認定的世界遺產。在這本相冊，讀者或許可以瞥見它們多彩的掠影。

新華社亞太總分社英文編輯部自 2019 年起開設"亞洲相冊"專欄，迄今發稿 1000 多組。這本書籍中，精選了 200 多張照片。

我們希望，此書能讓讀者"一卷在手，亞太萬千氣象盡在眼中"。動人的影像講述動人的亞太故事、動人的中國故事。希望讀者喜歡這部動人的故事。

《亞洲相冊》編委會

Preface

In the vast land of Asia-Pacific, more than 100 Xinhua journalists are at their posts every day, recording sunrise and rain, sweat and smiles, suffering and hope with lens and pen...

Our colorful "log" shows that an open and inclusive Asia-Pacific community of a shared future with innovative growth, connectivity and win-win cooperation is turning from concept to action, from vision to reality, showing vibrant vitality and bearing fruit.

The story we are telling you is the story of Asia, the story of Asia-Pacific, the story of China and Asia-Pacific, and the story of the Asia-Pacific community of a shared future. The main theme of the story is to lead the road of common development with Chinese-style modernization, drive the modernization process of Asia-Pacific countries, and move forward hand in hand towards the goal of building a community of a shared future for mankind.

We believe that such a grand narrative may sometimes be better proclaimed serenely and peacefully. Silent photographs can also play beautiful music in one's heart.

We hope that readers will turn the pages of this *Asia Album* as if they were walking between the magnificent rivers and mountains and colorful cities of Asia, sometimes feeling shocked, sometimes feeling heartfelt, and sometimes letting out a heartfelt smile.

The constant protagonist of images is people. From this album, we can see that the people of Asia work hard day after day in the fields and factories, supporting more than half of the global population; the festival of sprinkling, water festival, Eid...people in the diverse and colorful days of festivals and celebrations singing and dancing; the opening of the China-Laos Railway, the Jakarta-Bandung High Speed Railway put into operation... At these important historical moments, glory and dreams are written on their faces. Win-win cooperation is the road to development, and they are jointly promoting the wheels of economic development, guarding the common homeland, and moving forward on the road of green development.

It can also be seen that in the earthquake in Afghanistan, the tsunami in Tonga, when natural disasters are rampant, the people of Asia and the Pacific always watch out for each other.

Over the past 10 years, China and the countries under the Belt and Road Initiative have built a number of national landmarks and livelihood projects, and have reaped tangible and substantial results. Many landmark projects of the Belt and Road, such as airports, ports, highways, high-speed railways, light railways, power stations and industrial parks, have shown us that connectivity is the main line of the "Development Belt" and the "Road of Happiness" benefiting the people of all countries.

The Asia-Pacific region is rich in cultural and intangible heritage, many of which are recognized by UNESCO as World Heritage sites. In this photo album, readers may catch a glimpse.

The English editorial department of Xinhua News Agency's Asia-Pacific head office has launched the Asia Album column since 2019, and has so far sent out more than 1,000 sets of articles. In this book, more than 200 photos have been selected.

We hope that this book will give readers a glimpse of Asia and the Pacific in a single volume. Moving images tell a moving story of Asia-Pacific and a moving story of China. We hope readers will enjoy this moving story.

Editorial Committee of *Asia Album*

1
2
3
4
5
6
7
8

目　錄　Contents

一座橋、一條鐵路、一次握手……鏡頭下的那一刻留住了歷史中值得記錄的片段，它們凝聚著民眾的期待、希望和夢想，它們勾勒出亞太相互尊重、公平正義、合作共贏的大舞台。

A bridge, a railroad, a handshake...The moments caught on camera document the moments in history that are worth recording. They represent people's expectations, hopes and dreams, and the broad stage of mutual respect, fairness and justice, and win-win cooperation in the Asia-Pacific region.

1

歷史一刻
Moments in History

1-1

中國援建的柬埔寨國家體育場
是第 32 屆東南亞運動會的主要場館

2023 年 5 月 5 日，第 32 屆東南亞運動會在柬埔寨
首都金邊的國家體育場開幕。

On May 5, 2023, the 32nd Southeast Asian
Games opened at the National Stadium in Phnom
Penh, Cambodia.

1-1-1

2023 年 5 月 5 日，這是開幕式上的文藝表演。（新華社稿，索萬納拉攝）

Artists perform at the opening ceremony of the 32nd Southeast Asian (SEA) Games at the Morodok Techo
National Stadium in Phnom Penh, Cambodia on May 5, 2023. (Photo by Sovannara / Xinhua)

1-1-2

2023 年 5 月 5 日，這是開幕式上的文藝表演。（新華社稿，索萬納拉攝）

Artists perform at the opening ceremony of the 32nd Southeast Asian (SEA) Games at the Morodok Techo National Stadium in Phnom Penh, Cambodia on May 5, 2023. (Photo by Sovannara / Xinhua)

1-1-3

2023 年 5 月 17 日，這是閉幕式上的焰火表演。（新華社稿，索萬納拉攝）

Fireworks light up the sky over the Morodok Techo National Stadium during the closing ceremony of the 32nd Southeast Asian (SEA) Games in Phnom Penh, Cambodia, May 17, 2023. (Photo by Sovannara / Xinhua)

1-2

中國基建實現孟加拉國人民千百年夢想
歷時七年建成帕德瑪大橋

帕德瑪大橋位於達卡西南約 40 公里處，全長 9.8 公里，主橋長 6.15 公里，採用雙層鋼桁樑結構，上層為四車道公路，下層是單綫鐵路，由中國中鐵大橋局中標承建，創下中國企業承建的最大海外橋樑工程紀錄。

For Bangladeshis, a dream is coming true. The history of crossing the mighty Padma river between dozens of districts in southern Bangladesh and the capital of Dhaka only by ferries or boats is all set to end. The mega multipurpose road-rail bridge dubbed the "Dream Padma Bridge" of Bangladesh is nearing completion after workers overcame tons of hurdles, including challenges brought by the COVID-19 pandemic. The huge infrastructure, with the main bridge spanning 6.15 km in length, is undertaken by China Railway Major Bridge Engineering Group Co, Ltd (MBEC). It is the largest and most challenging infrastructure project in Bangladesh's history.

1-2-2

這是 2021 年 8 月 21 日在孟加拉國蒙希甘傑拍攝的帕德瑪大橋項目（無人機照片）。（新華社稿）

Photo taken on Sept. 12, 2021 shows a view of Padma Multipurpose Bridge Project under construction in Munshiganj on the outskirts of Dhaka, Bangladesh. (Xinhua)

1-2-1

2023 年 5 月 2 日，張亞東（右）在孟加拉國帕德瑪大橋鐵路連接綫項目上與孟加拉國員工交流。（新華社稿）

Zhang Yadong (R), an engineer from China Railway Group Limited, works with a Bangladeshi man on the Padma Bridge Rail Link Project in Dhaka, Bangladesh on May 2, 2023. (Xinhua)

I-2-3

這是 2021 年 9 月 12 日拍攝的正在
建設中的孟加拉國帕德瑪大橋。
（新華社稿）

Photo taken on Sept. 12, 2021 shows
a view of Padma Multipurpose
Bridge Project under construction in
Munshiganj on the outskirts of Dhaka,
Bangladesh. (Xinhua)

1-3

中國和新西蘭科考人員到達克馬德克海溝最深點

中國—新西蘭聯合深淵深潛科考隊 2022 年 11 月 27 日在新西蘭奧克蘭表示，首次中國—新西蘭聯合深淵深潛科考航次第一航段科考任務順利完成，兩國科考人員藉助載人潛水器到達克馬德克海溝最深點。

The China-New Zealand Joint Abyssal Deep Diving Team said in Auckland, New Zealand on Nov. 27, 2022, that the first segment of the first China-New Zealand Joint Abyssal Deep Diving Voyage has been successfully completed, and the researchers of the two countries have reached the deepest point of the Kermadec Trench with the help of manned submersibles.

1-3-1

2022 年 11 月 27 日，中國"探索一號"科考船搭載著"奮鬥者"號全海深載人潛水器停靠在新西蘭奧克蘭皇后碼頭。（新華社記者，郭磊攝）

China's research vessel Tansuoyihao loaded with the Human Occupied Vehicle Fendouzhe docks at Queens Wharf in Auckland, New Zealand, Nov. 27, 2022. (Xinhua / Guo Lei)

1-3-2

2022 年 11 月 4 日，在中國"探索一號"科考船上，中科院深海所潛航員鄧玉清（中）、袁鑫（左）
和新西蘭國家水資源和大氣研究所科研人員卡琳·施納貝爾準備進行萬米深潛。（新華社稿，中科院
深海所供圖，陳坤鑫攝）

Submersible pilots Deng Yuqing (C) and Yuan Xin (L) from China's Institute of Deep-Sea Science and Engineering
(IDSSE) of the Chinese Academy of Sciences, and New Zealand Marine biologist Dr. Kareen Schnabel from
the National Institute of Water and Atmospheric Research, prepare for their expedition to the Kermadec Trench
onboard China's research vessel Tansuoyihao, Nov. 4, 2022. (Chen Kunxin / IDSSE / Handout via Xinhua)

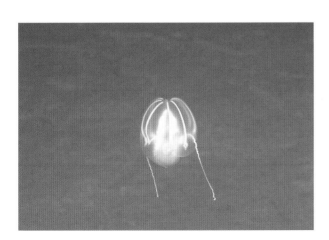

1-3-3

這是 2022 年 11 月 14 日 "奮
鬥者" 號在深海拍攝的海洋生
物。（新華社稿）

A marine organism is pictured
from Human Occupied Vehicle
Fendouzhe in deep sea on Nov. 14,
2022. (Xinhua)

1-4

中老鐵路帶火老撾旅遊景區　加速推進泛亞高鐵經濟圈

中老鐵路全長 1035 公里，於 2021 年 12 月 3 日開通運營，是"一帶一路"倡議與老撾"變陸鎖國為陸聯國"戰略對接的重要項目。

The China-Laos Railway connects Kunming in China's Yunnan Province with the Laotian capital Vientiane. The 1,035-km railway, a landmark project of high-quality Belt and Road cooperation, started operation on Dec. 3, 2021.

1-4-1

2022 年 7 月 19 日，我軍衛生列車通過中老友誼隧道內的兩國邊界。我軍赴老撾參加"和平列車—2022"活動的衛生列車 19 日上午從磨憨站駛出，通過"一隧連兩國"的友誼隧道後抵達老撾。這是中老鐵路開通以來，首次組織衛生列車跨境投送。（新華社稿，凱喬攝）

The medical train of the People's Liberation Army of China crosses the border with Laos by running through the Friendship Tunnel of China-Laos Railway, on July 19, 2022. A medical team of the People's Liberation Army of China has arrived in Laos to join the Lao People's Army to carry out the "Peace Train-2022" joint humanitarian medical rescue and services drills. (Photo by Kaikeo Saiyasane / Xinhua)

1-4-2

2022 年 12 月 1 日，中老友好農冰村小學的學生乘坐"瀾滄號"動車組欣賞中老鐵路老撾段沿綫風光。（新華社稿，凱喬攝）

Students from the China-Laos Friendship Nongping Primary School are seen on the Lane Xang EMU train in Laos, Dec. 1, 2022. (Photo by Kaikeo Saiyasane / Xinhua)

1-4-3

2023 年 4 月 13 日，在中老鐵路老撾萬象站，工作人員歡迎乘坐 D887 次國際旅客列車的旅客。（新華社記者，邢廣利攝）

Staff members welcome passengers taking the first cross-border passenger train from Kunming in southwest China's Yunnan Province to Lao capital Vientiane, at the Vientiane station of the China-laos Railway in Vientiane, Laos, April 13, 2023. The China-Laos Railway started cross-border passenger services on Thursday, a move that is expected to boost regional connectivity. (Xinhua / Xing Guangli)

1-4-4

2023 年 4 月 13 日，從老撾萬象站駛出的 D888 次列車行駛在雲南省西雙版納州境內的中老鐵路橄欖壩特大橋上。（新華社記者，單宇琦攝）

The first cross-border passenger train departing from the Lao capital Vientiane to Kunming, the capital of southwest China's Yunnan Province, runs on the Ganlanba bridge of the China-Laos railway in Xishuangbanna Dai Autonomous Prefecture in Yunnan Province, April 13, 2023. (Xinhua / Shan Yuqi)

1-5

中國印尼聯手打造東南亞首條高鐵 —— 雅萬高鐵

備受各界關注的雅萬高鐵於 2023 年 10 月 17 日正式開通運營。作為中印尼共建"一帶一路"合作的標誌性項目,雅萬高鐵連接印度尼西亞首都雅加達和旅遊名城萬隆,是中國高鐵首次全系統、全要素、全產業鏈在海外落地。這條最高運營時速 350 公里的高鐵,是印尼乃至東南亞的第一條高速鐵路。

雅萬高鐵全長 142 公里,全綫共有 13 座隧道、56 座橋樑,橋隧比例達 76%。中印尼兩國建設者們勇於攻堅克難,一同以高標準、高質量完成任務。雅萬高鐵通車後,將雅加達和萬隆間的通行時間從 3 個多小時縮短至 40 多分鐘。根據印尼中國高速鐵路有限公司數據,截至 23 年 12 月上旬,雅萬高鐵累計乘客數量已突破 70 萬人次,客流呈現強勁增長態勢。

這條在爪哇島上跋山涉水的"鋼鐵巨龍"擦亮了中國高鐵的金色名片,將中國高質量發展成果與印尼高質量發展願景緊密相連,為沿綫城市和民眾帶來加速奔向美好生活的新機遇。

The Jakarta-Bandung High-Speed Railway (HSR) jointly built by China and Indonesia was officially put into commercial operation on Tuesday.

The 142.3 km long high-speed line, connecting Jakarta and the fourth largest city Bandung, is a flagship project that synergizes the China-proposed Belt and Road Initiative and Indonesia's Global Maritime Fulcrum strategy.

It is also the first overseas construction project that fully uses Chinese railway systems, technology and industrial components.

In addition to greatly cutting the journey between the two cities from over three hours to around 40 minutes, Indonesia's Transportation Minister Budi Karya Sumadi told Xinhua in an interview that the Jakarta-Bandung HSR would greatly promote regional people-to-people exchanges and drive the development sectors including tourism, employment and education.

1-5-1

2023 年 9 月 13 日，在印度尼西亞雅加達，印度尼西亞總統佐科在哈利姆站和雅萬高鐵高速動車組合影。（新華社記者，徐欽攝）

Indonesian President Joko Widodo poses for photos with a high-speed electric multiple unit (EMU) train on the platform of Halim Station of the Jakarta-Bandung High-Speed Railway in Jakarta, Indonesia, Sept. 13, 2023. (Xinhua / Xu Qin)

1-5-2

2023 年 10 月 17 日，在印度尼西亞雅加達哈利姆站，乘務人員在站台歡迎乘客。當日，雅萬高鐵正式開通運營。（新華社記者，徐欽攝）

A crew member gestures to welcome passengers at the platform of Halim Station on the Jakarta-Bandung High-Speed Railway in Jakarta, Indonesia, Oct. 17, 2023. (Xinhua / Xu Qin)

1-5-3

2023 年 10 月 17 日，乘客在行駛中的雅萬高鐵高速動車組列車車廂內拍照。（新華社記者，徐欽攝）

Passengers take selfies in a carriage of a high-speed electrical multiple unit (EMU) train running on the Jakarta-Bandung High-Speed Railway in Indonesia, Oct. 17, 2023. (Xinhua / Xu Qin)

1-5-4

這是 2023 年 9 月 30 日在印度尼西亞普哇加達拍攝的一列行駛中的雅萬高鐵高速動車組（無人機照片）。（新華社記者，徐欽攝）

This aerial photo taken on Sept. 30, 2023 shows a high-speed electrical multiple unit (EMU) train of the Jakarta-Bandung High-Speed Railway running in Purwakarta, Indonesia. (Xinhua / Xu Qin)

1-6

民眾在阿富汗喀布爾機場爭相撤離

1-6-1

2021 年 8 月 24 日，人們在阿富汗首都喀布爾國際機場排隊等候乘坐德國軍用飛機離開。（新華社稿）

People queue up to board a military aircraft of Germany and leave Kabul at Kabul airport, Afghanistan, Aug. 24, 2021. (Xinhua)

1-6-2

這是 2021 年 8 月 27 日在阿富汗喀布爾機場附近拍攝的爆炸現場。阿富汗首都喀布爾國際機場外 26 日發生兩起爆炸。極端組織"伊斯蘭國"阿富汗分支宣稱發動襲擊。綜合阿富汗衛生部門和美國軍方消息，襲擊致使大量阿富汗平民和至少 13 名美軍士兵喪生。（新華社稿，塞夫拉赫曼‧薩菲攝）

Photo taken on Aug. 27, 2021 shows the explosion site near the Kabul airport in Afghanistan. The death toll from the Kabul airport attacks on Thursday has reportedly risen to at least 103. (Photo by Saifurahman Safi / Xinhua)

1-6-3

2021 年 8 月 27 日，一輛救護車停在阿富汗喀布爾機場附近的爆炸現場。（新華社稿，塞夫拉赫曼‧薩菲攝）

An ambulance is seen at the explosion site near the Kabul airport in Afghanistan, Aug. 27, 2021. (Photo by Saifurahman Safi / Xinhua)

1-7

第八批在韓中國人民志願軍烈士遺骸回國

2021 年 9 月 2 日上午，中國和韓國在韓國仁川國際機場共同舉行在韓中國人民志願軍烈士遺骸交接儀式。

South Korea on Thursday returned 109 more remains of Chinese People's Volunteers martyrs killed in the 1950-53 Korean War. The eighth repatriation ceremony was held at the Incheon International Airport, west of the capital Seoul.

1-7-1

2021 年 9 月 2 日，在韓國仁川國際機場，中國人民解放軍禮兵準備護送烈士棺椁登上解放軍空軍專機。（新華社記者，王婧嬌攝）

Chinese soldiers carry coffins containing remains of Chinese People's Volunteers martyrs killed in the 1950-53 Korean War during a repatriation ceremony at Incheon International Airport in Incheon, South Korea, Sept. 2, 2021. (Xinhua / Wang Jingqiang)

2021 年 9 月 2 日，在韓國仁川國際機場，中國人民解放軍禮兵（左）從韓方接過中國人民志願軍烈士棺椁。（新華社記者，王婧嬙攝）

Chinese soldiers (left row) receive coffins containing remains of Chinese People's Volunteers martyrs killed in the 1950-53 Korean War during a repatriation ceremony at Incheon International Airport in Incheon, South Korea, Sept. 2, 2021. (Xinhua / Wang Jingqiang)

2021 年 9 月 2 日，在韓國仁川國際機場，中國人民解放軍禮兵準備護送烈士棺椁登上解放軍空軍專機。（新華社記者，王婧嬙攝）

Chinese soldiers salute to coffins containing remains of Chinese People's Volunteers martyrs killed in the 1950-53 Korean War during a repatriation ceremony at Incheon International Airport in Incheon, South Korea, Sept. 2, 2021. (Xinhua / Wang Jingqiang)

1-8

慶香港回歸　賀國安立法

1-8-1

2020 年 7 月 1 日，香港特區政府在灣仔金紫荊廣場舉行升旗儀式，慶祝香港回歸祖國 23 週年。（新華社記者，李鋼攝）

A flag-raising ceremony is held by the government of the Hong Kong Special Administrative Region to celebrate the 23rd anniversary of Hong Kong's return to the motherland at the Golden Bauhinia Square in Hong Kong, south China, July 1, 2020. (Xinhua / Li Gang)

1-8-2

2020 年 6 月 30 日，香港市民在銅鑼灣街頭支持實施香港國安法。當日，十三屆全國人大常委會第二十次會議表決通過〈中華人民共和國香港特別行政區維護國家安全法〉，並決定將該法列入香港基本法附件三，由香港特別行政區在當地公佈實施。（新華社記者，王申攝）

Hong Kong citizens celebrate the passage of the Law of the People's Republic of China on Safeguarding National Security in the Hong Kong Special Administrative Region (HKSAR) in Causeway Bay of south China's Hong Kong. The law was passed at the 20th session of the Standing Committee of the 13th National People's Congress (NPC). (Xinhua / Wang Shen)

1-8-3

2023 年 7 月 1 日，載著 "慶香港回歸" 標語的船隻從香港維多利亞港駛過。當日，100 多艘漁船在香港維多利亞港巡遊，慶祝香港回歸祖國 23 週年。（新華社記者，呂小煒攝）

A ship carrying the slogan of "celebrating the 23rd anniversary of Hong Kong's return to the motherland" sails at the Victoria Harbour in Hong Kong, south China, July 1, 2020. In Victoria Harbor, 150 fishing vessels, festooned with banners and the national flag, sailed in a procession to celebrate the 23rd anniversary of Hong Kong's return to the motherland and the passage of the national security law. (Xinhua / Lui Siu Wai)

1-9

中國與基里巴斯復交、與所羅門群島建交

2019 年 9 月 27 日，國務委員兼外交部長王毅（右）在紐約中國常駐聯合國代表團同基里巴斯共和國總統兼外長馬茂握手。當日，國務委員兼外交部長王毅在紐約中國常駐聯合國代表團同基里巴斯共和國總統兼外長馬茂簽署〈中華人民共和國與基里巴斯共和國關於恢復外交關係的聯合公報〉。（新華社記者，劉傑攝）

Chinese State Councilor and Foreign Minister Wang Yi (R) and Kiribati's President and Foreign Minister Taneti Mamau shake hands at the Chinese Permanent Mission to the United Nations in New York, Sept. 27, 2019. Wang Yi and Taneti Mamau signed a document to restore the diplomatic relations between the two countries here on Friday. (Xinhua / Liu Jie)

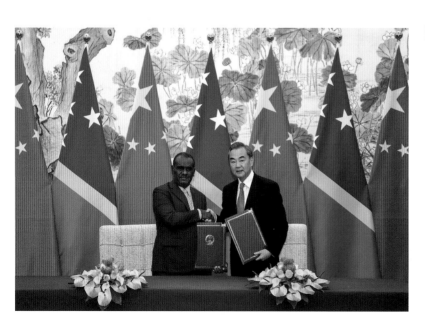

2019 年 9 月 21 日，國務委員兼外交部長王毅同所羅門群島外長馬內萊在北京舉行會談並簽署〈中華人民共和國和所羅門群島關於建立外交關係的聯合公報〉。（新華社記者，謝環馳攝）

Chinese State Councilor and Foreign Minister Wang Yi and Solomon Islands' Minister of Foreign Affairs and External Trade Jeremiah Manele sign a joint communique on the establishment of diplomatic relations after their talks in Beijing, capital of China, Sept. 21, 2019. (Xinhua / Xie Huanchi)

1-10

中國領導人赴印尼泰國出席 G20 峰會、APEC 峰會

1-10-1

這是 2022 年 11 月 12 日在印度尼西亞巴厘島拍攝的峰會主會場外的峰會標識。二十國集團領導人第十七次峰會即將在印度尼西亞巴厘島舉行。（新華社記者，王益亮攝）

Photo taken on Nov. 12, 2022 shows the logo for the upcoming 17th Group of 20 (G20) Summit outside Apurva Kempinski, the main venue for the summit in Bali, Indonesia. (Xinhua / Wang Yiliang)

1-10-2

這是 2022 年 11 月 16 日在泰國首都曼谷街頭拍攝的 2022 年亞太經合組織會議標識。亞太經合組織第二十九次領導人非正式會議將於 11 月 18 日至 19 日在泰國曼谷舉行。（新華社記者，王騰攝）

A logo of APEC 2022 is pictured on a street in Bangkok, Thailand, Nov. 16, 2022. The 29th Asia-Pacific Economic Cooperation (APEC) Economic Leaders' Meeting will be held in Bangkok, Thailand, on Nov. 18-19. (Xinhua / Wang Teng)

1-11

新冠疫情下的東京奧運會

2021 年 8 月 5 日，美國選手克勞瑟奪得東京奧運會田徑項目男子鉛球冠軍後，在胸前展示寫有 "祖父，我們做到了，2020 奧運會冠軍！" 字樣的紙條。（新華社記者，李一博攝）

Ryan Crouser of the United States displays a message after winning the men's shot put final at Tokyo 2020 Olympic Games, in Tokyo, Japan, Aug. 5, 2021. (Xinhua / Li Yibo)

2021 年 7 月 24 日，楊倩在頒獎儀式上。當日，在東京奧運會射擊女子 10 米氣步槍決賽中，中國選手楊倩奪冠，贏得東京奧運會首枚金牌。（新華社記者，鞠煥宗攝）

Gold medalist Yang Qian of China gestures during the awarding ceremony for the women's 10m air rifle event at the Tokyo 2020 Olympic Games in Tokyo, Japan, July 24, 2021. (Xinhua / Ju Huanzong)

2021 年 8 月 6 日，中國隊第四棒吳智強（左三）和第三棒蘇炳添（左四）在比賽中。當日，在東京奧運會田徑男子 4×100 米接力決賽中，中國隊獲得第四名。（新華社記者，賈宇辰攝）

Wu Zhiqiang (3rd L) and Su Bingtian (4th L) of China compete during the men's 4×100m relay final at Tokyo 2020 Olympic Games, in Tokyo, Japan, Aug. 6, 2021. (Xinhua / Jia Yuchen)

1-11-4

2021 年 8 月 5 日，東
京奧運會田徑項目女
子七項全能選手在比
賽後合影（高空遙控
相機照片）。（新華社
記者，張傳奇攝）

Athletes pose for a
photo with the Olympic
rings after the women's
heptathlon at Tokyo
2020 Olympic Games,
in Tokyo, Japan, Aug. 5,
2021. (Xinhua / Zhang
Chuanqi)

2023 年是 "一帶一路" 倡議提出十週年。十年來，中國與共建 "一帶一路" 國家打造了一個個 "國家地標" 與 "民生工程"，收穫了實打實、沉甸甸的成果。機場、港口、公路、高鐵、輕軌、電站和工業園等眾多 "一帶一路" 標誌性項目，展示了共建 "一帶一路" 以互聯互通為主綫，已成為造福世界的 "發展帶" 和惠及各國人民的 "幸福路"。

The year of 2023 marks the 10th anniversary of the Belt and Road Initiative (BRI). Over the past 10 years, China and participating countries have achieved fruitful results by jointly building national landmarks and livelihood projects.

Airports, ports, highways, high-speed railways, light rails, power plants and industrial parks constructed under the BRI have boosted connectivity. The BRI has become a belt of socio-economic development and a road to happiness for various countries and their peoples.

2

一帶一路
The Belt and Road Initiative

2-1

馬爾代夫：中馬友誼大橋

由中資公司承建的中馬友誼大橋是馬爾代夫首座跨海大橋，連接首都馬累和隔海相望的胡魯馬累島，大橋於 2018 年 8 月 30 日正式通車。這座兩公里長的大橋是馬爾代夫和中國合作共建 "21 世紀海上絲綢之路" 的標誌性項目之一，它讓當地人和遊客來往馬累和胡魯馬累的時間縮短至 5 分鐘。

The China-Maldives Friendship Bridge, the first cross-sea bridge in the Maldives built by a Chinese company connecting the Maldivian capital of Male with neighboring Hulhule Island, was inaugurated on Aug. 30, 2018.

The 2-km-long bridge is an iconic project of the Maldives and China in co-building the 21st Century Maritime Silk Road. The bridge makes it possible for locals and tourists to travel between the two islands within five minutes.

2-1-1
2018 年 8 月 31 日，馬爾代夫新婚夫婦在中馬友誼大橋上舉行浪漫的集體婚禮。（新華社記者，唐璐攝）

Maldivian couples attend a mass wedding ceremony on the China-Maldives Friendship Bridge in Male, the Maldives on Aug. 31, 2018. (Xinhua / Tang Lu)

2-1-2

2018 年 8 月 31 日，一對馬爾代夫新婚夫婦在中馬友誼大橋上舉行浪漫的集體婚禮。（新華社記者，唐璐攝）

A Maldivian couple attend a mass wedding ceremony on the China-Maldives Friendship Bridge in Male, the Maldives on Aug. 31, 2018. (Xinhua / Tang Lu)

2-1-3

這是 2019 年 9 月 1 日拍攝的中馬友誼大橋（無人機照片）。（新華社稿，王明亮攝）

Aerial photo taken on Sept. 1, 2019 shows the China-Maldives Friendship Bridge in Maldives. (Photo by Wang Mingliang / Xinhua)

2-1-4

這是 2018 年 8 月 22 日拍攝的中馬友誼大橋（無人機照片）。（新華社稿，王明亮攝）

Photo taken on Aug. 22, 2018 shows a view of the China-Maldives Friendship Bridge in the Maldives. (Photo by Wang Mingliang / Xinhua)

2-2

斯里蘭卡：科倫坡港口城和漢班托塔港

科倫坡港口城是斯里蘭卡與中國 "一帶一路" 合作旗艦項目，通過填海造地方式在科倫坡商業區旁建造一座新城。項目建成後將成為南亞地區集商業、金融、住宅和娛樂等為一體的高端城市綜合體。

On reclaimed land adjacent to the commercial district of Colombo, the Colombo Port City is a flagship joint project between Sri Lanka and China within the framework of the Belt and Road Initiative (BRI). It aims to be a commercial, financial, residential and international entertainment hub in South Asia.

2-2-1

這是 2020 年 9 月 23 日拍攝的科倫坡港口城建設工地（無人機照片）。（新華社稿，科倫坡港口城項目公司供圖）

Aerial photo taken on Sept. 23, 2020 shows a view of the construction site of the Colombo Port City in Colombo, Sri Lanka. (China's CHEC Port City Colombo (Pvt) Ltd. / Handout via Xinhua)

2-2-2

2020 年 9 月 22 日，工人正在科倫坡港口城建設工地施工。（新華社記者，唐璐攝）

People work at the construction site of the Colombo Port City in Colombo, Sri Lanka, Sept. 22, 2020. (Xinhua / Tang Lu)

2-2-3

這是 2021 年 11 月 30 日拍攝的科倫坡港口城建設工地。（新華社記者，唐璐攝）

Photo taken on Nov. 30, 2021 shows a construction site at the Colombo's Port City in Sri Lanka. (Xinhua / Tang Lu)

2-2-4

這是 2019 年 12 月 14 日拍攝的斯里蘭卡漢班托塔港（無人機照片）。（新華社稿，劉鴻儒攝）
Aerial photo taken on Dec. 14, 2019 shows the Hambantota International Port in Sri Lanka. (Photo by Liu Hongru / Xinhua)

漢班托塔港位於斯里蘭卡南部海岸，距離印度洋主航道僅有 10 海里，是"一帶一路"的重要樞紐之一。

Sitting on the southern coast of Sri Lanka, Hambantota Port is only 10 nautical miles from the busy shipping routes on the Indian Ocean and is an important junction along the Belt and Road.

2-2-5

這是 2019 年 12 月 14 日拍攝的在斯里蘭卡漢班
托塔港停靠的一艘滾裝船和滾裝碼頭（無人機照
片）。(新華社稿，劉鴻儒攝)

Aerial photo taken on Dec. 14, 2019 shows a roll-
on/roll-off (RORO) ship and RORO yard at the
Hambantota International Port in Sri Lanka. (Photo by
Liu Hongru / Xinhua)

2-3

柬埔寨：中柬合作金港高速公路和暹粒吳哥國際機場

金港高速公路連接柬埔寨首都金邊和該國深水國際港西哈努克港，是柬埔寨的首條高速公路，極大促進了該國的經濟增長和旅遊業發展。金港高速公路由中國路橋公司投資，在經過3年多的建設後，於2022年10月1日通車。

Connecting the Cambodian capital of Phnom Penh to the international deep-sea port province of Preah Sihanouk, the Phnom Penh-Sihanoukville Expressway, the first expressway in Cambodia, has been giving a significant boost to the country's economic growth and tourism development.

Invested by the China Road and Bridge Corporation, the freeway was opened to traffic on Oct 1, 2022 after more than three years of construction.

2-3-1

2022年11月7日，柬埔寨金港高速公路收費站的工作人員向一名過路司機發放電子通行證。（新華社記者，吳長偉攝）

A staff member presents an e-pass for traveling on the Phnom Penh-Sihanoukville (PPSHV) Expressway to a driver in Phnom Penh, Cambodia on Nov. 7, 2022. (Xinhua / Wu Changwei)

2-3-2

這是 2022 年 10 月 8 日拍攝的車輛在柬埔寨金港高速公路金邊收費站排隊等候（無人機照片）。（新華社稿，柬埔寨金港高速公路有限公司供圖）

This photo taken on Oct 8, 2022 shows vehicles lining up at a toll station on the Phnom Penh-Sihanoukville Expressway in Phnom Penh, Cambodia. (PPSHV Expressway / Handout via Xinhua)

暹粒吳哥國際機場距被列入聯合國教科文組織世界遺產名錄的吳哥窟約 40 公里，距暹粒市區約 50 公里，是中柬"一帶一路"合作的重點項目。這座由中國企業投資建設的機場位於柬埔寨西北部暹粒省，於 2023 年 11 月 16 日正式投入運營。

The Siem Reap Angkor International Airport, about 40 km from the UNESCO listed Angkor Archaeological Park and 50km from Siem Reap provincial town, is a landmark project of cooperation between Cambodia and China under the Belt and Road Initiative(BRI). The Chinese-invested airport in northwest Cambodia's Siem Reap province was officially inaugurated on Nov. 16, 2023.

2-3-3

2023 年 11 月 16 日，一架客機抵達柬埔寨暹粒吳哥國際機場。（新華社稿，廖泓清攝）

A passenger plane arrives at the Siem Reap Angkor International Airport (SAI) in Siem Reap province, Cambodia, Nov. 16, 2023. (Photo by Liao Hongqing / Xinhua)

2-3-4

2023 年 11 月 16 日，旅客在柬埔寨暹粒吳哥國際機場等候航班。（新華社稿，廖泓清攝）

Passengers wait for their flights at the Siem Reap Angkor International Airport (SAI) in Siem Reap province, Cambodia, Nov. 16, 2023. (Photo by Liao Hongqing / Xinhua)

2-4

孟加拉國：卡納普里河底隧道

由中國企業承建的孟加拉國和南亞地區首條水下隧道——孟加拉國卡納普里河底隧道項目 2023 年 10 月 28 日正式通車。這條隧道將把未來的亞洲高速路與達卡—吉大港—科克斯巴扎爾高速路連接起來，同時將吉大港至東南部港口城市科克斯巴扎爾之間的路程縮短 40 公里。

The Bangabandhu Sheikh Mujibur Rahman Tunnel, a Chinese-built underwater tunnel, the first in Bangladesh and South Asia, was inaugurated on Oct 28, 2023. The tunnel will connect the proposed Asian Highway to Dhaka-Chattogram-Cox's Bazar Highway and will reduce the distance from Chattogram to the southeastern seabeach town Cox's Bazar by 40 km.

2-4-1

2023 年 10 月 29 日，在孟加拉國吉大港市，車輛通過卡納普里河底隧道。（新華社稿）

This photo taken on Oct 29, 2023 shows the Bangabandhu Sheikh Mujibur Rahman Tunnel in Chattogram, Bangladesh. (Xinhua)

2-4-2

2023 年 10 月 29 日，在孟加拉國吉大港市，車輛通過卡納普里河底隧道。（新華社稿）

This photo taken on Oct 29, 2023 shows the Bangabandhu Sheikh Mujibur Rahman Tunnel in Chattogram, Bangladesh. (Xinhua)

2-5

巴基斯坦：瓜達爾港、塔爾煤田和卡洛特水電站

瓜達爾港位於巴基斯坦西南部的俾路支省。作為
中巴經濟走廊的重要項目之一，瓜達爾港的建設
和運營近年來取得了重要進展。瓜達爾港從一個
落後的小漁村正發展成為"巴基斯坦的深圳"，
這座城市現在不僅擁有港口、自由區和商業中
心，更重要的是擁有良好的發展繁榮前景。

中巴經濟走廊於 2013 年啟動建設，是兩國"一
帶一路"合作的旗艦項目。中巴經濟走廊南起瓜
達爾港北至中國西北部的新疆喀什，以港口、能
源、運輸、產業合作為重點。

The Gwadar port in Pakistan's southwestern
Balochistan province has made great progress
in its construction and operation over the
years as a leading project of the CPEC. From
a small, remote and less developed fishing
village, the port now is embracing its new
identity of Pakistan's "Shenzhen" with fully
functional port terminal, free zone, business
center and, more importantly, a visible future
of development and prosperity.

Launched in 2013, CPEC, the flagship
project of the China-proposed Belt and Road
Initiative, is a corridor linking the Gwadar port
in southwestern Pakistan with Kashgar in
northwest China's Xinjiang Uygur Autonomous
Region, which highlights energy, transport and
industrial cooperation.

2-5-3

2018 年 1 月 29 日，人們參加巴基斯坦瓜達爾自由區開園儀式。（新華社稿，艾哈邁德‧卡邁勒攝）

People attend the inauguration ceremony of the first phase of Gwadar Port's Free Zone in southwest Pakistan's Gwadar on Jan. 29, 2018. (Xinhua / Ahmad Kamal)

2-5-1

這是 2023 年 12 月 4 日拍攝的位於巴基斯坦西南部的瓜達爾港。（新華社記者，唐斌輝攝）

This photo taken on Dec. 4, 2023 shows a view of the Gwadar port in southwest Pakistan's Gwadar. (Xinhua / Tang Binhui)

2-5-2

這是 2018 年 1 月 29 日拍攝的位於巴基斯坦西南部的瓜達爾港。（新華社稿，艾哈邁德‧卡邁勒攝）

Photo taken on Jan. 29, 2018 shows a view of Gwadar Port in southwest Pakistan's Gwadar. (Xinhua / Ahmad Kamal)

2-5-4

這是 2023 年 3 月 21 日拍攝的巴基斯坦塔爾煤田一區塊煤電一體化項目。塔爾煤田一區塊煤電一體化項目中的燃煤電站位於巴基斯坦南部信德省，是中巴經濟走廊框架下的能源合作項目。這座燃煤電站 2023 年 2 月初正式投入商業運營，其發電量可以滿足 400 萬戶家庭的用電需求。（新華社稿，艾哈邁德‧卡邁勒攝）

This photo taken on March 21, 2023 shows the view of Thar Coal Block-I Coal Electricity Integration project in Sindh province, Pakistan. The Thar Coal Block-I Coal Electricity Integration project, an energy cooperation project in Pakistan's southern Sindh province under the framework of the China-Pakistan Economic Corridor (CPEC), was officially put into commercial operation in early February 2023. It has the capacity to fulfill the electricity demand of 4 million households in Pakistan. (Xinhua / Ahmad Kamal)

這是 2022 年 4 月 9 日在巴基斯坦東部旁遮普省航拍的卡洛特水電站項目。卡洛特水電站是中巴經濟走廊重要水電投資項目，2022 年 6 月全面投入商業運營。其將為巴基斯坦提供清潔廉價的電力，促進巴綠色發展。（新華社稿，中國三峽集團供圖）

Aerial photo taken on April 9, 2022 shows a view of the Karot Hydropower Project in Punjab province, eastern Pakistan. The hydropower plant, a major pilot project under the China-Pakistan Economic Corridor (CPEC), was put into full commercial operation in June 2022. It will generate environment-friendly and cheap electricity, promoting green development in Pakistan. [China Three Gorges Corporation (CTG) / Handout via Xinhua]

2-6

緬甸：皎漂港中緬油氣管道

作為"一帶一路"倡議在緬甸實施的先導項目，中緬油氣管道項目於 2010 年 6 月開工，包括原油管道項目和天然氣管道項目。其中天然氣管道於 2013 年投產運行，隨後在 2017 年原油管道也正式投產運行。

As pioneer projects of China's Belt and Road Initiative (BRI), the China-Myanmar oil and gas pipeline project began in June 2010, with the aim of transporting natural gas and crude oil from the west coast of Myanmar to China. By 2013 and 2017 respectively, the two pipelines were fully operational.

2-6-1

2020 年 1 月 13 日，中石油工程師張永斌在緬甸皎漂馬德島中緬油氣管道項目現場檢查。（新華社記者，杜宇攝）

Engineer Zhang Yongbin from China National Petroleum Corporation (CNPC) checks the pipeline at the China-Myanmar oil and gas pipeline project in Kyaukpyu, Rakhine State, Myanmar on Jan. 13, 2020 (Xinhua / Du Yu)

2020 年 1 月 13 日，一艘油輪停靠在緬甸皎漂馬德島中緬油氣管道項目卸油碼頭，準備卸載石油（無人機拍攝）。（新華社記者，杜宇攝）

Photo taken on Jan. 13, 2020 shows an oil tanker at a terminal of the China-Myanmar oil and gas pipeline project in Kyaukpyu, Rakhine State, Myanmar. (Xinhua / Du Yu)

2-7

馬來西亞：東海岸鐵路和馬中關丹工業園

馬來西亞東海岸鐵路項目是中馬兩國共建"一帶一路"重點項目，全長 600 多公里，被視為連通馬來西亞東西海岸的"陸上橋樑"，建成後有望帶動馬來西亞東海岸地區經濟發展，並極大改善沿綫地區互聯互通水平。

馬中關丹產業園是中國在馬來西亞設立的首個國家級產業園區，也是"一帶一路"規劃重大項目和跨境國際產能合作示範基地。馬中關丹產業園於 2013 年正式開園，與中馬欽州產業園組成中馬"兩國雙園"，是中馬兩國領導人直接倡議和推動的重大合作項目。

The East Coast Rail Link (ECRL) is a major infrastructure project under the Belt and Road Initiative (BRI) with a total planning length of over 600km, running from Malaysia's largest transport hub Port Klang and travels across the peninsula to Kelantan state in northeastern Malaysia. The rail link is expected to greatly enhance connectivity and bring more balanced growth to the country upon its completion.

The Malaysia-China Kuantan Industrial Park (MCKIP), the first industrial park jointly developed by Malaysia and China, is a key Belt and Road cooperation project and a demonstration base for cross-border industrial capacity cooperation. The MCKIP, launched in 2013, together with the China-Malaysia Qinzhou Industrial Park situated in China, has set an innovative example of bilateral economic cooperation under the model of "Two Countries, Twin Parks."

這是 2023 年 4 月 26 日在馬來西亞吉蘭丹州拍攝的馬來西亞東海岸鐵路項目一分部製樑場（無人機照片）。（新華社記者，朱煒攝）

This aerial photo taken on April 26, 2023 shows a beam yard of the East Coast Rail Link (ECRL), a major infrastructure project under the Belt and Road Initiative (BRI) in Kelantan, Malaysia. (Xinhua / Zhu Wei)

2023 年 4 月 26 日，工人在馬來西亞吉蘭丹州的馬來西亞東海岸鐵路項目一分部製樑場工作。（新華社記者，朱煒攝）

Employees work at a beam yard of the East Coast Rail Link (ECRL), a major infrastructure project under the Belt and Road Initiative (BRI) in Kelantan, Malaysia, April 26, 2023. (Xinhua / Zhu Wei)

圖為 2019 年 4 月 15 日拍攝的馬來西亞馬中關丹產業園聯合鋼鐵項目（無人機照片）。（新華社記者，朱煒攝）

Photo taken on April 15, 2019 shows the Alliance Steel at the Malaysia-China Kuantan Industrial Park in Pahang, Malaysia. (Xinhua / Zhu Wei)

2-8

越南：河內輕軌

河內吉靈—河東綫輕軌使用中國政府優惠貸款，採用中國設備、技術和標準，由中國中鐵六局集團有限公司負責承建，是越南首個城市輕軌項目，也是中越兩國共建"一帶一路"基礎設施領域合作的標誌性項目。

The Cat Linh-Ha Dong urban railway line, Vietnam's first urban railway, is a symbolic cooperation project between Vietnam and China in the field of infrastructure to jointly build the Belt and Road Initiative (BRI). The railway is funded by Chinese official development aid (ODA) and constructed by China Railway Sixth Group Co. Ltd.

2-8-1

2023 年 12 月 9 日，列車在越南河內吉靈—河東輕軌綫上行駛。（新華社記者，程一恆攝）

A train runs on the Cat Linh-Ha Dong urban elevated railway in Hanoi, Vietnam, Dec. 9, 2023. (Xinhua / Cheng Yiheng)

2-8-2

2023 年 6 月 23 日，一列輕軌列車在越南首都河內吉靈—河東綫上行駛。（新華社稿，范挺德攝）

Photo taken on June 23, 2023 shows a train running on the Cat Linh-Ha Dong urban railway line in Hanoi, capital of Vietnam. (Photo by Pham Dinh Duc / Xinhua)

2-9

泰國：羅勇工業園

在中泰共建 "一帶一路" 的引領下，泰中羅勇工業園成立於 2006 年，是中國首批境外經貿合作區之一。目前工業園已吸引了 180 家中國製造企業、30 多家配套企業在泰投資，為當地提供超過 4.5 萬個就業崗位。

The Thai-Chinese Rayong Industrial Zone in Rayong Province of Thailand, established in 2006, is one of China's first overseas economic and trade cooperation zones as well as China's first overseas industrial park developed and built in Thailand under China's Belt and Road Initiative (BRI), which is home to more than 180 Chinese-invested companies, and has attracted more than 4.3 billion U.S. dollars in investment from China and provided more than 45,000 local jobs.

2-9-1

2022 年 11 月 8 日，在位於泰國羅勇府的泰中羅勇工業園，泰國工程師那塔武在盾安金屬（泰國）有限公司生產綫上工作。（新華社稿，拉亨攝）

Natawut Lorboon works at the production line of Dunan Metals (Thailand) Co., Ltd, in the Thai-Chinese Rayong industrial zone in Rayong Province, Thailand, Nov. 8, 2022. (Photo by Rachen Sageamsak / Xinhua)

2-9-2

這是 2021 年 12 月 29 日在泰國羅勇府拍攝的泰中羅勇工業園（無人機照片）。（新華社記者，王騰攝）

Aerial photo taken on Dec. 29, 2021 shows the Thai-Chinese Rayong Industrial Zone in Rayong province, Thailand. (Xinhua / Wang Teng)

2-9-3

2021 年 12 月 29 日，工作人員在位於泰國羅勇府的泰中羅勇工業園工作。（新華社記者，王騰攝）

A worker checks tube bundles at the Thai-Chinese Rayong Industrial Zone in Rayong province, Thailand, Dec. 29, 2021. (Xinhua / Wang Teng)

2-10

老撾：中老鐵路

中老鐵路是高質量共建"一帶一路"的標誌工程，也是中國"一帶一路"倡議與老撾"變陸鎖國為陸聯國"戰略的對接項目。它北起中國雲南昆明，南至老撾首都萬象，全長1035公里。自2021年12月3日正式開通運營以來，為當地人帶來了巨大收益。

The China-Laos Railway is a landmark project showcasing high-quality Belt and Road cooperation. The railway also serves as a docking project with Laos' strategy to convert itself from a landlocked country to a land-linked hub. Since its launch in December 2021, the 1,035-km rail line, which links the Lao capital Vientiane with Kunming, the capital of southwest China's Yunnan Province, has delivered benefits more than just at local levels.

2-10-1

2023年4月13日，老撾工作人員在中老鐵路上由雲南開往老撾首都萬象的國際旅客列車上表演。（新華社記者，邢廣利攝）

Lao staff members perform at the first cross-border passenger train from Kunming in southwest China's Yunnan Province to Lao capital Vientiane on April 13, 2023. (Xinhua / Xing Guangli)

2-10-2

2022 年 11 月 25 日，"瀾滄號"動車組列車在老撾萬象郊區的中老鐵路上行駛。（新華社稿，凱喬攝）

This aerial photo taken on Nov. 25, 2022 shows a Lane Xang EMU (electric multiple unit) train running on the China-Laos Railway in the suburb of Vientiane, Laos. (Photo by Kaikeo Saiyasane / Xinhua)

2-11

印尼：雅萬高鐵

全長 142.3 公里的雅萬高鐵是中印尼共建"一帶一路"合作的標誌性項目，連接印度尼西亞首都雅加達和旅遊名城萬隆。雅萬高鐵於 2023 年 10 月 17 日正式開通運營，這條最高運營時速 350 公里的高鐵，是印尼乃至東南亞的第一條高速鐵路。

The 142.3-km-long Jakarta-Bandung High-Speed Railway, connecting Indonesia's capital city Jakarta and the fourth largest city Bandung, is a flagship project that synergizes the China-proposed Belt and Road Initiative. The high-speed line, the first of its kind with a design speed of 350 km/h in Indonesia and Southeast Asia, was officially put into commercial operation on Oct 17, 2023.

2-11-1

2023 年 11 月 5 日，在印度尼西亞雅加達哈利姆站，人們和雅萬高鐵高速動車合影。（新華社記者，徐欽攝）

People pose for photos with a high-speed train of the Jakarta-Bandung High-Speed Railway at Halim Station in Jakarta, Indonesia, Nov. 5, 2023. (Xinhua / Xu Qin)

2-11-2

這是 2023 年 10 月 16 日在印度尼西亞帕達拉朗拍攝的一列行駛中的雅萬高鐵高速動車組（無人機照片）。（新華社記者，徐欽攝）

This photo taken on Oct 16, 2023 shows a high-speed electrical multiple unit (EMU) train running on the Jakarta-Bandung High-Speed Railway in Padalarang, Indonesia. (Xinhua / Xu Qin)

在亞太這個人口眾多、經濟繁榮的大家庭，人們無時無刻不感受著它的多樣性，從民族、種族、宗教習俗，再到文化禮儀，也正是這樣的多元色彩繪成了亞太的絢麗多姿。在這裏，你能看到各種自然奇觀，感歎於大自然的鬼斧神工。在街頭巷尾，你也可以品嚐特色小吃，和當地人聊上幾句，怎能不感到放鬆愜意？來吧，來看看多姿多彩的亞太吧。

Welcome to the vigorous and vibrant Asia-Pacific, where you can find diversified cultures and unique wonders of nature and historical spots. In immersively experiencing rich cultures across the region, locally made gourmet could satisfy your taste and local people could invite you for a cup of tea, so you will be the king of the world.

3

大千世界
Dynamic Lifestyles

3-1

阿富汗

3-1-1

2022 年 6 月 2 日阿富汗坎大哈省，一名教師正在流動課堂授
課。（新華社稿，薩努拉－塞拉米攝）

A teacher gives a lesson at a "mobile school" in Kandhar province,
Afghanistan, June 2, 2022. A "mobile school" has been set up in
Kandhar province of Afghanistan. The "mobile school" travels from
village to village to provide education chances for local kids. (Photo by
Sanullah Seiam / Xinhua)

3-1-2

2022 年 6 月 2 日阿富汗坎大哈省，一名兒童正在流動課堂朗讀。（新華社稿，薩努拉－塞拉米攝）

A girl reads during a class at a "mobile school" in Kandhar province, Afghanistan, June 2, 2022. (Photo by Sanullah Seiam / Xinhua)

3-1-3

2023 年 9 月 25 日阿富汗首都喀布爾，工作人員正在為一名兒童接種預防小兒麻痺疫苗。（新華社稿，塞夫拉赫曼・薩菲攝）

A health worker gives a dose of anti-polio vaccine to a child in Kabul, Afghanistan, Sept. 25, 2023. (Photo by Saifurahman Safi / Xinhua)

3-1-4

2022 年 12 月 9 日阿富汗法拉省，兩名男子正在參加摔跤比賽。（新華社稿，馬沙爾攝）

Participants take part in a wrestling competition in Farah province, Afghanistan, Dec. 9, 2022. (Photo by Mashal / Xinhua)

3-2

澳大利亞

3-2-1

2022 年 9 月 17 日，澳大利亞一年一度規模最大的迎春活動——堪培拉花展在聯邦公園拉開帷幕。（新華社稿，儲晨攝）

Photo taken on Sept. 17, 2022 shows the festival event of Floriade at the Commonwealth Park in Canberra, Australia. Floriade, one of the Australian Capital Territory's signature events, opened in the Commonwealth Park on Saturday for the first time in three years with the theme Sounds of Spring. Hundreds of thousands of people are expected to flood into the festival event. (Photo by Chu Chen / Xinhua)

3-2-2

2022 年 9 月 17 日澳大利亞首都堪培拉的聯邦公園，遊客正在自拍。（新華社稿，儲晨攝）

Visitors take a selfie at the festival event of Floriade in the Commonwealth Park in Canberra, Australia, Sept. 17, 2022. (Photo by Chu Chen / Xinhua)

3-3

孟加拉國

3-3-1

2023 年 2 月 24 日孟加拉國達卡，一名貓咪主人在貓咪展上懷抱貓咪。（新華社稿）

A cat owner holds his cat during a cat ramp show in Dhaka, Bangladesh on Feb. 24, 2023. (Xinhua)

3-3-2

2023 年 9 月 2 日孟加拉國吉大港魚市。（新華社稿）

This photo taken on Sept. 2, 2023 shows baskets full of fish at a market in Bangladesh's seaport city of Chattogram. (Xinhua)

3-3-3

2022 年 5 月 20 日孟加拉國蘭加馬蒂水上市場。（新華社稿）

A boat loaded with fruits is seen at a floating market in Rangamati, Bangladesh, on May 20, 2022. (Xinhua)

3-3-4

2022 年 10 月 25 日孟加拉國博里薩爾，農民划船查看水上蔬菜種植基地。（新華社稿）

Farmers row boats beside floating vegetable beds in Barisal, Bangladesh, Oct. 25, 2022. (Xinhua)

3-4

印度

3-4-1
2022 年 3 月 24 日印度新德里，模特在時裝週上展示印度服裝設計師瓦伊沙莉的作品。（新華社稿，賈維德・達爾攝）

A model displays a creation by Indian designer Vaishali S during the FDCI × Lakmé Fashion Week in New Delhi, India, March 24, 2022. (Photo by Javed Dar / Xinhua)

3-4-2
2022 年 3 月 25 日印度新德里，模特在時裝週上展示印度服裝設計師馬尼什的作品。（新華社稿，賈維德・達爾攝）

Models display creations by Indian designer Manish Malhotra during the FDCI × Lakmé Fashion Week in New Delhi, India, March 25, 2022. (Photo by Javed Dar / Xinhua)

2023 年 7 月 6 日印度博帕爾，
騎車的人們將頭部包裹以遮陽防
曬。（新華社稿）

A woman rides with her head covered
from the sun during hot summer in
Bhopal, capital of India's Madhya
Pradesh state, July 6, 2023. (Xinhua)

2023 年 5 月 7 日印度特里普拉
邦，民眾用微笑迎接世界微笑
日。（新華社稿）

People laugh during a laughter
session on "World Laughter Day" at
Agartala, the capital city of India's
northeastern state of Tripura, May 7,
2023. (Xinhua)

3-5

老撾

3-5

2023 年 3 月 14 日老撾萬象夜市，
一名商販正在烹飪食物。（新華社
稿，凱喬攝）

A vendor prepares food at a night
market in Vientiane, Laos, March 14,
2023. (Photo by Kaikeo Saiyasane /
Xinhua)

3-6

馬來西亞

3-6-1

2022 年 5 月 18 日,在馬來西亞雪蘭莪州,一名男子正在製作拉茶。

拉茶是馬來西亞最普遍和最受歡迎的國民飲料之一。拉茶的主要成分是茶葉和煉乳,其製作過程是使用兩個大的茶缸,把沖泡好的茶水與煉乳混合後來回多次的從高處往下倒,動作猶如將茶湯在兩個茶缸間來回拉,這樣可以使茶水和煉乳的混合更為充分。拉得越長,起泡越多,茶香與奶香越能獲得充分的發揮,味道也會更加順滑。(新華社稿,張紋綜攝)

Photo taken on May 18, 2022 shows a man making Teh tarik in Selangor's Petaling Jaya, Malaysia. (Photo by Chong Voon Chung / Xinhua)

3-6-2

2023 年 8 月 23 日，在馬來西亞吉隆坡附近的馬來西亞國家動物園，大熊貓"興興"準備享用生日大餐。

在馬來西亞國家動物園大熊貓保護中心內，中國旅馬大熊貓夫婦"興興"和"靚靚"23 日迎來了 17 歲生日。當天馬來西亞國家動物園為這對同日出生的大熊貓夫婦舉行了盛大的慶生儀式。（新華社稿，張紋綜攝）

Giant panda Xing Xing enjoys birthday treats at the Giant Panda Conservation Center in Zoo Negara near Kuala Lumpur, Malaysia, Aug 23, 2023. (Photo by Chong Voon Chung / Xinhua)

3-6-3

2023 吉隆坡塔國際跳傘節於 2023 年 2 月 3 日至 5 日在馬來西亞吉隆坡舉行，眾多跳傘愛好者從吉隆坡塔上一躍而下。（新華社稿，張紋綜攝）

Participants leap from the Kuala Lumpur Tower during the annual Kuala Lumpur Tower International Jump event in Kuala Lumpur, Malaysia, Feb. 3, 2023. This 3-day event kicked off here on Friday. (Photo by Chong Voon Chung / Xinhua)

3-7

新西蘭

3-7-1

2022 年 9 月 29 日，在新西蘭首都惠靈頓世界可穿戴藝術大賽現場，模特展示設計作品。

世界可穿戴藝術大賽是新西蘭乃至南半球一年一度的設計盛典。其設計理念以跨界、超現實、時空交錯和奇思怪想而著稱。（新華社記者，郭磊攝）

A model presents a creation during the 2022 World of WearableArt (WOW) in Wellington, New Zealand, Sept. 29, 2022. The Awarding Night of 2022 WOW, a renowned international design competition, was held here on Friday. (Xinhua / Guo Lei)

3-7-2

2022 年 9 月 29 日，在新西蘭首都惠靈頓世界可穿戴藝術大賽現場，模特展示設計作品。

世界可穿戴藝術大賽是新西蘭乃至南半球一年一度的設計盛典。其設計理念以跨界、超現實、時空交錯和奇思怪想而著稱。（新華社記者，郭磊攝）

A model presents a creation during the 2022 World of WearableArt (WOW) in Wellington, New Zealand, Sept. 29, 2022. The Awarding Night of 2022 WOW, a renowned international design competition, was held here on Friday. (Xinhua / Guo Lei)

3-8

巴基斯坦

2022 年 8 月 18 日巴基斯坦南部城市卡拉奇，模特在新娘時裝週上展示特色服飾。（新華社稿）

A model presents a creation during a bridal festival fashion show in southern Pakistani port city of Karachi on Aug. 18, 2022. (Xinhua)

3-8-2
2023 年 10 月 15 日巴基斯坦拉合爾街頭，廚師正在製作美食。（新華社稿，薩賈德攝）

Chefs cook food at a stall by the street in Lahore, Pakistan, Oct. 15, 2023. (Photo by Sajjad / Xinhua)

3-8-3
2023 年 1 月 8 日巴基斯坦南部城市卡拉奇，一名新娘在集體婚禮現場化妝。（新華社稿）

A bride gets making up during a mass wedding ceremony in southern Pakistani port city of Karachi on Jan. 8, 2023. (Xinhua)

3-8-4
2023 年 11 月 12 日巴基斯坦卡拉奇海灘，人們在欣賞落日。（新華社稿，艾哈邁德·卡瑪爾攝）

This photo taken on Nov. 12, 2023 shows the silhouette of people viewing sunset at a beach in Karachi, south Pakistan. (Photo by Ahmad Kamal / Xinhua)

3-9

菲律賓

3-9-1

2020 年 12 月 6 日，在菲律賓馬尼拉，人們乘坐貢多拉在 "水上電影院" 觀看電影。（新華社稿，烏馬利攝）

Visitors on board gondolas (traditional flat-bottomed Venetian rowing boats) watch a movie at the "floating cinema" in Manila, the Philippines, Dec. 6, 2020. A floating cinema was launched in a local mall as indoor cinemas all over the country are still closed due to the COVID-19 pandemic. (Photo by Rouelle Umali / Xinhua)

3-9-2

2022 年 3 月 14 日菲律賓奎松市，一名女消防員正在參加女消防員競技大賽。（新華社稿，烏馬利攝）

A female firefighter participates in the Women Firefighters Skills Olympics at the Philippine Bureau of Fire Protection-National Capital Region (BFP-NCR) headquarters in Quezon City, the Philippines on March 14, 2022. (Photo by Rouelle Umali / Xinhua)

3-10

新加坡

2023 年 5 月 8 日，遊客（右）在新加坡飛禽公園餵鳥。當日，新加坡飛禽公園開放首日迎來遊客。（新華社稿，鄧智煒攝）

A tourist (R) reacts while feeding birds on the first day of the soft launch of the Bird Paradise in Singapore, on May 8, 2023. (Photo by Then Chih Wey / Xinhua)

2023 年 5 月 8 日，遊客在新加坡飛禽公園觀賞飛禽表演。（新華社稿，鄧智煒攝）

Tourists watch the "Predators on Wings" show on the first day of the soft launch of the Bird Paradise in Singapore, on May 8, 2023. (Photo by Then Chih Wey / Xinhua)

3-11

韓國

3-11

2023 年 5 月 26 日韓國釜山，遊客正在海雲台沙灘欣賞沙雕。（新華社記者，王益亮攝）

Tourists view a sand sculpture at Haeundae Beach in Busan, South Korea, May 26, 2023. (Xinhua / Wang Yiliang)

3-12

斯里蘭卡

3-12-1

2022 年 5 月 29 日，一對母女在斯里蘭卡首都科倫坡舉行的 "母女時裝設計師大賽" 中展示休閒裝。

當日，2022 年度 "母女時裝設計師大賽" 在科倫坡舉行。十名服裝設計師展示了自己設計的休閒裝、運動裝和晚裝。最引人注目的是，比賽中的所有時裝展示都是由設計師本人和她們的媽媽一起完成的。(新華社稿，阿吉特・佩雷拉攝)

Models present creations during the Mother Daughter fashion show in Colombo, Sri Lanka, on May 29, 2022. The highlight of the show is that the designs are modeled by real mother-daughter duos. (Photo by Ajith Perera / Xinhua)

3-12-2

2023 年 10 月 3 日，遊客在斯里蘭卡加勒體驗高蹺海釣。

高蹺海釣是具有斯里蘭卡特色的一種海釣方式，漁人坐在一根矗立在海中的高高的木棍上，掌握好平衡和支撐的同時使用魚竿釣魚。(新華社稿，阿吉特・佩雷拉攝)

Tourists try stilt fishing in Galle, Sri Lanka, Oct. 3, 2023.

Stilt fishing is a method of fishing unique to the island country of Sri Lanka. Local fishermen sit on a crossbar called "petta", which is tied to a vertical pole driven into the sand a few meters offshore. From that position, a fisherman will cast his rod and wait until a fish takes the bait. (Photo by Ajith Perera / Xinhua)

3-13

泰國

3-13-1

2022 年 6 月 26 日，參賽者在泰國春武里府駕馭水牛參加比賽。春武里府當天舉行賽牛節，展示當地傳統農耕文化。（新華社稿，拉亨攝）

Buffalo racers compete during the annual Buffalo Race in Chonburi, Thailand, on June 26, 2022. (Photo by Rachen Sageamsak / Xinhua)

3-13-2

2022 年 1 月 5 日，在泰國沙沒頌堪府美功縣，一輛列車通過美功鐵道市場。

美功鐵道市場位於泰國中部沙沒頌堪府美功縣，每天都有列車從美功火車站開出穿梭於市場間。附近商販們將攤位鋪設在鐵軌兩邊，在火車即將抵達前收起，等待火車從自己面前不足一米處緩緩駛過。這樣的景象為鐵道市場吸引了眾多遊客。新冠疫情後，旅客數量減少，穿梭於此的列車從每天八班減少為兩班。附近的商販們依舊堅守在鐵軌旁，等待市場恢復昔日的熱鬧。（新華社記者，王騰攝）

A commuter train runs through Maeklong Railway Market in Samut Songkhram Province, Thailand, Jan. 5, 2022. In Maeklong Railway Market, built along a railway track, a compromise is reached between vendors and passing commuter trains. When the rail track is clear, stall owners can set up stalls at will. Before the COVID-19 pandemic, the market had attracted many tourists. Nowadays, due to the decrease of passengers, the number of trains that shuttle here every day has been reduced from eight to two. (Xinhua / Wang Teng)

2023 年 8 月 5 日，瑜伽愛好者在泰國曼谷梵高光影展上練習瑜伽。（新華社稿，拉亨攝）

Yoga enthusiasts practice yoga at the Van Gogh Alive Event in Bangkok, Thailand, Aug. 5, 2023. (Photo by Rachen Sageamsak / Xinhua)

3-14

越南

這是 2023 年 7 月 22 日在越南河內一家咖啡店拍攝的繪製河內風光圖案的雞蛋咖啡。越南特色飲品雞蛋咖啡由蛋黃、糖、煉乳和咖啡等原料製成，其獨特的風味受到當地民眾和外國遊客喜愛。（新華社稿，范挺德攝）

This photo taken on July 22, 2023 shows egg coffee with patterns of Hanoi's landscape at a coffee shop in the Old Quarter in Hanoi, capital of Vietnam. (Photo by Pham Dinh Duc / Xinhua)

2023 年是中國提出“親誠惠容”周邊外交理念十週年，“親”體現在親仁善鄰；“誠”體現在以誠相待；“惠”體現在互惠互利；“容”體現在開放包容。中國與亞太各國的親密交往涵蓋文化、醫療、農業、基礎設施、體育、人道主義救援等諸多方面，一張張現場照片以及照片背後的故事，呈現出一個“可信、可愛、可敬”的中國。

The year 2023 marks the 10th anniversary of China's principle of amity, sincerity, mutual benefit and inclusiveness in neighborhood diplomacy.

Featuring specific events of close interaction between China and Asia-Pacific countries, the collection covers culture, health care, agriculture, infrastructure, sports, humanitarian relief and other aspects. Through the photos directly on the scene and the stories behind, we hope to present China's image as "credible, lovely and respectable", and illustrates the diplomatic concept.

4

親誠惠容

Amity, Sincerity, Mutual Benefit and Inclusiveness

4-1

"和平方舟"醫療船訪問斐濟

4-1-1

2018 年 8 月 2 日，在斐濟蘇瓦港碼頭，軍樂隊奏響迎賓曲歡迎中國海軍和平方舟醫院船到訪。當地時間 8 月 2 日，執行"和諧使命—2018"任務的中國海軍和平方舟醫院船抵達斐濟蘇瓦港，開始為期 8 天的友好訪問並提供人道主義醫療服務。（新華社稿，江山攝）

Fiji military band performs to welcome the Chinese naval hospital ship Ark Peace, at the port of Suva Harbour, Suva, Fiji, on Aug. 2, 2018. The Chinese naval hospital ship Ark Peace, which is on Mission Harmony-2018, arrived on Thursday in the Fijian capital city of Suva, beginning an eight-day goodwill visit and providing humanitarian medical service in Fiji. (Photo by Jiang Shan / Xinhua)

4-1-2

2018 年 8 月 2 日，中國海軍和平方舟醫院船緩緩駛抵斐濟蘇瓦港。（新華社稿，江山攝）

Chinese naval hospital ship Ark Peace arrives at the Suva Harbour, Suva, Fiji, on Aug. 2, 2018. (Photo by Jiang Shan / Xinhua)

4-2

中國軍艦為湯加運送海嘯救援物資

2022 年 1 月 28 日，赴湯加執行運送救災物資任務海上運輸編隊官兵在裝載救災物資（無人機照片）。由兩艘中國人民解放軍海軍艦艇組成的艦隊 1 月 31 日從中國廣州出發，向南太平洋島國湯加運送中國的救災物資。在湯加遭受大規模火山噴發和隨之而來的海嘯襲擊後，中國已向湯加提供了多批緊急救援物資。最新的供應品重約 1400 噸，包括移動房屋、拖拉機、發電機、水泵、淨水器、食品和醫療用品。（新華社稿，殷徵攝）

Aerial photo taken on Jan. 28, 2022 shows relief supplies being transferred onto a ship waiting to depart for Tonga, in Guangzhou, south China's Guangdong Province.

A flotilla comprised of two ships of the People's Liberation Army (PLA) Navy departed from a port in south China's Guangzhou City on Jan. 31, 2022 to deliver China's disaster relief supplies to the South Pacific island nation of Tonga.

This relief mission follows China's delivery of multiple batches of emergency supplies to Tonga, which was hit by disasters resulting from a massive volcano eruption earlier this month and its ensuing tsunami.

Weighing approximately 1,400 tonnes, the latest supplies include mobile homes, tractors, electricity generators, water pumps, water purifiers, food and medical supplies. (Photo by Yin Zheng / Xinhua)

2022 年 1 月 26 日，中國空軍運 -20 飛機在廣州白雲機場裝載運往湯加的救災物資（手機照片）。（新華社記者，丁增義攝）

Photo taken with a mobile phone shows disaster relief materials loaded onto two Chinese air force transport aircrafts to head for Tonga at the Guangzhou Baiyun International Airport in Guangzhou, south China's Guangdong Province, Jan. 26, 2022. (Xinhua / Ding Zengyi)

4-3

印尼紀念鄭和到訪該國 618 週年

4-3-1

這是 2023 年 8 月 29 日在印度尼西亞三寶壟拍攝的三保洞。(新華社記者，徐欽攝)

This photo taken on Aug. 29, 2023 shows a view of Sam Poo Kong, a place to commemorate Chinese Ming Dynasty navigator Zheng He, in Semarang, capital of Central Java province in Indonesia. (Xinhua / Xu Qin)

4-3-2

這是 2023 年 8 月 29 日在印度尼西亞三寶壟三保洞內拍攝的鄭和雕像。三寶壟是印度尼西亞中爪哇省的首府，也是印尼知名海港城市，中國明代航海家鄭和下西洋時曾在這裏登陸。(新華社記者，徐欽攝)

This photo taken on Aug. 29, 2023 shows a statue of Chinese Ming Dynasty navigator Zheng He at Sam Poo Kong in Semarang, capital of Central Java province in Indonesia. Zheng commanded expeditionary voyages to Southeast Asia, South Asia, Western Asia, and East Africa from 1405 to 1433. Semarang is one of several ports in Java visited by him in his seven expeditions to the Western Ocean. (Xinhua / Xu Qin)

4-4

中國風電項目助力泰國綠色能源轉化

4-4-1 & 4-4-2

這是 2023 年 10 月 5 日在泰國猜也蓬府拍攝的由中國金風科技提供的風力發電機（無人機照片）。猜也蓬風電場擁有 32 台中國金風風力渦輪機，總容量為 80 兆瓦，運營商隸屬於泰國最大的國有電力公司泰國電力局。（新華社記者，王騰攝）

This aerial photo taken on Oct. 5, 2023 shows China's Goldwind wind turbines in Chaiyaphum, Thailand. The Chaiyaphum wind farm hosts 32 of China's Goldwind wind turbines with a total capacity of 80 MW and is operated by EGCO, a major energy producer affiliated to the largest state utility Electricity Generating Authority of Thailand. (Xinhua / Wang Teng)

4-5

中國提供種子、機器
幫助孟加拉國農業發展

4-5-1

這是 2023 年 11 月 12 日在孟加拉國諾爾辛迪拍攝的古拉紹—布拉什化肥廠項目。該項目由中國化學工程第七建設有限公司與日本三菱重工合作承建，於 2020 年開始建設，是孟加拉國首個可回收利用二氧化碳的綠色化肥廠。（新華社稿）

This photo taken on Nov. 12, 2023 shows the Ghorashal-Polash Urea Fertilizer Project in Narsingdi, Bangladesh. Bangladeshi Prime Minister Sheikh Hasina has inaugurated the South Asian country's largest and first-ever green fertilizer factory as construction work of the Ghorashal-Polash Urea Fertilizer Project is completed.

Construction of the project started in 2020, and the China National Chemical Engineering & Construction Corporation Seven Ltd. (CC7), in collaboration with its Japanese partner Mitsubishi Heavy Industries (MHI), had been striving for the mega project to be completed as scheduled. (Xinhua)

4-5-2

2022 年 5 月 17 日，孟加拉國尼爾法馬里，一名農民在稻田裏收割水稻。"蒙加"是孟加拉語彙，農民用它來表示貧窮和富足永恆的年度循環。當季節合適時，所有人都有充足食物。當事情艱難時，每個人都會受苦。中國種子對孟加拉國實現大米生產自給自足至關重要。（新華社稿）

A farmer harvests rice in a paddy field in Nilphamari, Bangladesh, on May 17, 2022. "Monga" is a Bengali term farmers use for the eternal annual cycle of poverty and plenty. When the season is right, there is plenty for all. When things are tough, everyone suffers. Chinese seed is vital to Bangladesh's ambition to be self-sufficient in rice production. (Xinhua)

4-6

孟加拉國 "中國文化之夜"

4-6-1 & 4-6-2

2023 年 3 月 4 日，昆明國家歌舞劇院和孟加拉國的藝術家們在孟加拉國達卡舉行的中孟文化藝術之夜上表演。本次中孟文化藝術之夜由中國駐孟加拉國使館主辦、昆明國家歌舞劇院承辦，孟加拉國希爾帕卡拉學院（孟加拉國國家美術與表演藝術學院）支持。（新華社稿）

Artists of Kunming National Song & Dance Theater and artists of Bangladesh perform during the China-Bangladesh Culture & Art Night in Dhaka, Bangladesh, March 4, 2023. The China-Bangladesh Culture & Art Night, organized by the Chinese embassy in Bangladesh, was presented by Kunming National Song & Dance Theater, with the support of Bangladesh Shilpakala Academy or BSA (the Bangladeshi national academy of fine and performing arts). (Xinhua)

4-7

中國麵人藝術作品展在日本舉行

4-7-1

2020 年 1 月 17 日，在日本東京日中友好中心博物館，參觀者在麵塑展預展上欣賞麵塑藝術作品。展覽於 2020 年 1 月 18 日至 2 月 8 日舉行。（新華社記者，杜瀟逸攝）

Visitors enjoy dough modelling art works during the preview of Chinese dough modelling exhibition at Japan-China Friendship Center Museum in Tokyo, Japan, Jan. 17, 2020. The exhibition was held from Jan. 18 to Feb. 8, 2020. (Xinhua / Du Xiaoyi)

4-7-2

2020 年 1 月 17 日，在日本東京日中友好中心博物館，參觀者在麵塑藝術作品預展上觀看中國藝術家製作麵塑藝術作品。（新華社記者，杜瀟逸攝）

Visitors watch a Chinese artist creating a dough modelling art work during the preview of Chinese dough modelling exhibition at Japan-China Friendship Center Museum in Tokyo, Japan, Jan. 17, 2020. (Xinhua / Du Xiaoyi)

4-8

大熊貓在新加坡

4-8-1

2021 年 8 月 19 日，大熊貓 "嘉嘉" 在新加坡河川生態園抱著剛出生的熊貓寶寶。新加坡野生動物保育集團 15 日宣佈，中國旅新大熊貓 "嘉嘉" 14 日誕下首隻大熊貓寶寶 "叻叻"。（新華社稿，新加坡野生動物保育集團供圖）

Giant panda Jia Jia cradles its newborn cub in Singapore's River Safari on Aug. 19, 2021. Singapore saw the first giant panda birth on its land on Aug. 14, said a statement from the Wildlife Reserves Singapore (WRS) Group. (Wildlife Reserves Singapore Group / Handout via Xinhua)

4-8-2

2023 年 8 月 14 日，在新加坡河川生態園，大熊貓 "叻叻" 在兩歲生日慶祝活動上進食。"叻叻" 是新加坡首隻本土出生的大熊貓。（新華社稿，鄧智煒攝）

Giant panda Le Le, the first giant panda born in Singapore, enjoys food at its second birthday party held in Singapore's River Wonders, on Aug. 14, 2023. (Photo by Then Chih Wey / Xinhua)

4-9

馬來西亞舉行賽跑紀念中馬建交 49 週年

4-9-1 & 4-9-2

2023 年 11 月 12 日，人們在馬來西亞沙巴州哥打基納巴盧參加馬中誼跑活動。當日，"2023 馬中誼跑" 在馬來西亞沙巴州首府哥打基納巴盧舉行。此次活動旨在紀念中馬建交 49 週年，吸引約 3000 名民眾參與。（新華社記者，程一恆攝）

People participate in the Malaysia-China 2023 friendship run in Kota Kinabalu, Sabah, Malaysia, Nov. 12, 2023. About 3,000 people participated in the event to celebrate the 49th anniversary of the establishment of diplomatic relations between Malaysia and China. (Xinhua / Cheng Yiheng)

4-10

菲律賓的中醫教育和中醫推廣

2021 年 10 月 23 日，在菲律賓曼達盧永市，菲律賓岐黃中醫學院院長鄭啟明（右二）和全體教職員工出席了該研究院的揭牌儀式。該院是菲律賓衛生部認可的中醫教育機構，正式開設中醫在線課程，以推廣中醫，培養和培訓當地合格的中醫醫生。（新華社稿，烏馬利攝）

Philippine Qi Huang Traditional Chinese Medicine Institute (PQHTCMI) Executive Dean Zheng Qiming (2nd R) and faculty members are seen during the opening ceremony of the PQHTCMI in Mandaluyong City, the Philippines on Oct. 23. 2021. The PQHTCMI, a traditional Chinese medicine (TCM) education establishment recognized by the Philippine Department of Health, has officially opened and started its online course to promote the TCM, cultivate and train local qualified TCM practitioners. (Photo by Rouelle Umali / Xinhua)

2023 年 11 月 14 日，在菲律賓首都馬尼拉，人們在第二十屆世界中醫藥大會上參觀醫藥產品。第二十屆世界中醫藥大會 14 日在菲律賓首都馬尼拉開幕。為期兩天的大會以"人人享有健康，推動傳統醫學融入全球衛生健康治理"為主題，就中醫藥傳承與創新、中西醫結合等議題展開交流。（新華社稿，烏馬利攝）

People visit the 20th World Congress of Chinese Medicine in Manila, the Philippines, Nov. 14, 2023. The 20th World Congress of Chinese Medicine kicked off in the Philippine capital Manila, under the theme of "Health for all: integration of traditional medicine into universal health care." (Photo by Rouelle Umali / Xinhua)

4-11

新疆"木卡姆"在印尼演出

2023 年 7 月 19 日，在印度尼西亞雅加達，新疆藝術劇院木卡姆藝術團演員表演舞蹈《花腰帶》。當日，新疆藝術劇院木卡姆藝術團在印度尼西亞首都雅加達的伊斯梅爾·祖基公園演出。（新華社記者，徐欽攝）

Dancers from China's Xinjiang Art Theater Muqam Art Troupe perform in Taman Ismail Marzuki in Jakarta, Indonesia, July 19, 2023. Dozens of dancers and singers from China's Xinjiang Art Theater Muqam Art Troupe enlivened the stage of Taman Ismail Marzuki, the art center here in Indonesia's capital on Wednesday night. (Xinhua / Xu Qin)

2023 年 7 月 27 日，在印度尼西亞西爪哇省萬隆，新疆藝術劇院木卡姆藝術團演員進行表演。（新華社稿，塞提安賈爾攝）

Acrobats of China's Xinjiang Art Theater Muqam Art Troupe perform in Bandung, Indonesia, July 27, 2023. The art troupe presented its first performance in Jakarta, capital of Indonesia, on July 19, and will travel to other cities until August 10. (Photo by Septianjar Muharam / Xinhua)

4-12

中國為阿富汗提供人道主義援助

4-12-1

2023 年 10 月 15 日，中國政府援助阿富汗第一批抗震救災物資運抵阿西北部赫拉特省赫拉特市。兩架中國飛機運抵的救災物資主要是帳篷和摺疊床。阿富汗西北部先後發生兩次 6.2 級地震，超過 2000 人遇難，數千人受傷。地震發生後，中國政府第一時間決定向阿富汗提供緊急人道主義援助。（新華社稿，塞夫拉赫曼・薩菲攝）

The first batch of earthquake relief supplies donated by the Chinese government arrive at Herat International Airport in Herat province, Afghanistan, Oct. 15, 2023. Relief materials, including tents and rollaway beds, were unloaded from two Chinese cargo planes at the airport. Two deadly quakes, each with a magnitude of 6.2, followed by several aftershocks, rocked west Afghanistan with an epicenter in the Zanda Jan district of Herat province on Oct. 7, and left at least 2,000 dead and thousands more injured. (Photo by Saifurahman Safi / Xinhua)

4-12-2

2023 年 12 月 3 日，人們在阿富汗赫拉特省搬運中國捐贈的帳篷。一名政府官員表示，阿富汗西部赫拉特省 280 多戶受災家庭收到了中國捐贈的帳篷。（新華社稿，馬沙爾攝）

People transfer China-donated tents in Herat Province, Afghanistan, Dec. 3, 2023. Over 280 quake-affected families in west Afghanistan's Herat Province have received tents donated by China, said a government official. (Photo by Mashal / Xinhua)

4-13

中國為柬埔寨提供新冠疫苗

2022 年 3 月 29 日，中國援柬埔寨新冠疫苗運抵金邊。載有中國向柬埔寨無償援助的新一批新冠疫苗的飛機抵達金邊，以供柬埔寨開展疫苗第三劑加強針計劃。（新華社稿，李萊攝）

Photo taken on March 29, 2022 shows packages of Sinovac COVID-19 vaccine at the Phnom Penh International Airport in Phnom Penh, Cambodia. A plane carrying another batch of China-donated Sinovac COVID-19 vaccine arrives in the capital of Cambodia amid the country's booster shots vaccination drive. (Photo by Ly Lay / Xinhua)

2021 年 11 月 17 日，工作人員在柬埔寨金邊國際機場運輸中國援柬新冠疫苗。當日，柬埔寨政府在金邊國際機場舉行隆重儀式，迎接中國援柬新冠疫苗。柬埔寨首相洪森等到機場迎接。（新華社稿，批隆攝）

Workers unload China's Sinovac COVID-19 vaccines at the Phnom Penh International Airport in Phnom Penh, Cambodia, Nov. 17, 2021. The vaccine arrival was greeted by Cambodian Prime Minister Samdech Techo Hun Sen at the Phnom Penh International Airport. (Photo by Phearum / Xinhua)

亞太地區佔世界人口三分之一，佔世界經濟總量超過六成、貿易總量近一半，是全球經濟最具活力的增長帶，也是新冠疫情後全球經濟增長動力之源。經歷了疫情考驗的亞太各國努力振作恢復的同時，更結合綠色可持續發展的新經濟形勢，走出一條符合自己國情的發展道路。從 APEC 會議到"進博會"，從〈區域全面經濟夥伴關係協定〉到"一帶一路"項目，在充滿活力的亞太，你可以感受到世界經濟脈搏最有力的跳動。

The Asia-Pacific is the powerhouse of global economic growth, particularly in the post-COVID era, as the region is home to one third of the world's population and accounts for over 60% of the world's economy and nearly half of world's trade.

While recovering from the pandemic, Asia-Pacific countries have forged a development path suited to their national conditions in light of the new economic situation of green and sustainable development.

At the APEC meeting, China put forward its own proposal on continuing the "Asia-Pacific miracle", with Chinese modernization having brought opportunities and inspiration to the development of the region and the world at large.

The high-quality implementation of the Belt and Road Initiative and the Regional Comprehensive Economic Partnership Agreement has also tightened the economic ties between China and others countries in this dynamic region, where you can feel the strongest "heartbeats" of the world's economy.

經濟脈動
Economic Pulse

5-1

東盟國家的新能源產業發展勢頭可喜：探訪上汽正大泰國汽車工廠

5-1-1

2023 年 9 月 7 日，在位於泰國春武里府的上汽正大公司汽車工廠，工人在生產車間內工作。

由中國上汽集團與泰國正大集團合資的上汽正大有限公司泰國工廠於 2017 年竣工。該工廠位於泰國春武里府，佔地面積約 70 萬平方米，是上汽正大旗下 MG 品牌汽車在東南亞地區的生產製造基地。該公司目前也開始在泰國生產電動汽車。（新華社記者，王騰攝）

Workers work at the SAIC Motor-CP manufacturing plant in Chonburi, Thailand, Sept. 7, 2023.

As early as 2013, Chinese car manufacturer SAIC teamed up with Charoen Pokphand Group to found SAIC Motor-CP, a joint venture, in its bid to develop the vast market in the Association of Southeast Asian Nations (ASEAN) countries. The manufacturing plant, covering about 700,000 square meters, was completed in 2017. It is the manufacturing base of MG brand cars in Southeast Asia. SAIC Motor-CP also begins to production of electric vehicles. (Xinhua / Wang Teng)

5-1-2

2023 年 9 月 8 日，在位於泰國春武里府的上汽正大公司汽車工廠，工人進行車輛質量檢查。（新華社記者，王騰攝）

A worker works at the SAIC Motor-CP manufacturing plant in Chonburi, Thailand, Sept. 8, 2023. (Xinhua / Wang Teng)

5-2

中泰合作水上光伏項目助力泰國邁向低碳社會

5-2-1

這是 2022 年 12 月 8 日在泰國烏汶府詩琳通水庫拍攝的浮體光伏項目（無人機照片）。

在距離泰國首都曼谷 600 多公里的烏汶府詩琳通水庫上，七個碩大的藍色方形"島嶼"在陽光映照下熠熠生輝。這是中泰兩國聯合修建、泰國目前最大的浮體光伏項目。自 2021 年 10 月投入商業運營以來，這些中國製造的電池板不斷將日光轉化為清潔電能，輸送至千家萬戶。（新華社記者，王騰攝）

This aerial photo taken on Dec. 8, 2022 shows the floating solar farm at the Sirindhorn Dam in Ubon Ratchatani, Thailand. The hydro-floating solar project, located in the Sirindhorn Dam in northeastern Thailand, has now become a popular tourist spot with an exhibition center and a 400-meter-long "Nature Walkway". With an average net energy output of nearly 90 million kwh per year, the project has achieved its goal of providing low-cost, highly stable, eco-friendly energy. (Xinhua / Wang Teng)

5-2-2

2022 年 12 月 8 日，一名工作人員在泰國烏汶府詩琳通水庫巡查浮體光伏項目。（新華社記者，王騰攝）

A staff member inspects the floating solar farm at the Sirindhorn Dam in Ubon Ratchatani, Thailand, Dec. 8, 2022. (Xinhua / Wang Teng)

5-3

孟加拉國首個水上漂浮太陽能光伏發電站

5-3-1 & 5-3-2

2023 年 6 月 5 日，在孟加拉國查帕伊諾瓦布甘傑，工作人員檢查水上漂浮太陽能光伏發電站運行情況。

孟加拉國首個水上漂浮太陽能光伏發電站近日成功接入國家電網，該電站位於該國西部的查帕伊諾瓦布甘傑地區。（新華社稿，薩利姆攝）

A staff member checks the condition of the solar panels at a floating commercial solar power plant in Chapainawabganj district, some 302 km northwest of the capital Dhaka, Bangladesh, June 5, 2023.

In a major step towards expanding the country's solar energy production, the power plant, Bangladesh's first floating commercial solar power project, was connected to the national grid in 2023. (Photo by Salim / Xinhua)

5-4

RCEP 助力東盟國家農產品出口

5-4-1

2023 年 9 月 18 日，在泰國春蓬府一處果園內，工人在碼放剛採摘的榴蓮。泰國商務部數據顯示，2022 年，中國是泰國榴蓮最大出口市場，佔總出口量 96%，出口總額 30.9 億美元。

榴蓮在東南亞地區被稱為"水果之王"。在中國，榴蓮憑藉豐富的口感與獨特的風味，愈發受到消費者的認可與喜愛，但其高昂的價格也讓一些人望而卻步。

近年來，隨著〈區域全面經濟夥伴關係協定〉（RCEP）紅利釋放，中國—東盟自貿區建設深入推進，以及西部陸海新通道等一批互聯互通項目的建設，中國—東盟貿易規模進一步擴大。2023 年前 5 個月，廣西自東盟進口榴蓮突破 32.4 億元，同比增長 516%。依託中國—東盟博覽會等平台，越來越多東盟國家的榴蓮得以更加便捷地進入中國市場，並以更加優惠的價格走上消費者的餐桌。（新華社記者，王騰攝）

Workers load freshly harvested durians at an orchard in Chumphon, Thailand, Sept. 18, 2023. According to data from Thailand's Ministry of Commerce, China was the largest export market for Thai durians in 2022, accounting for more than 96 percent of the total export volume. As the vast majority of durians sold in the Chinese market are imported from Southeast Asia, the "king of fruits" has emerged as a prominent symbol of the booming China-ASEAN cooperation and China's vast market potential.

The flow of goods in this regional market has continued to benefit from tariff-free policies and expanded market access under the frameworks of the China-ASEAN Free Trade Area and the Regional Comprehensive Economic Partnership (RCEP).

In the first five months of 2023, Guangxi imported 3.66 billion yuan worth of fruits from ASEAN countries, a marked rise of 194 percent year on year. Among the most notable increases is durian, which surged 516 percent from the same period last year, according to customs data. (Xinhua / Wang Teng)

5·4·2

2023 年 9 月 15 日，在越南多樂省一家榴蓮果園，一名果農初步清潔剛採摘的榴蓮。

多樂省是越南榴蓮的主產地之一，眼下當地榴蓮已進入採摘季節，一批批從樹上採摘的新鮮榴蓮陸續運達加工廠，工人們投入到緊張的分揀、處理、包裝和發貨工作中。（新華社稿，范挺德攝）

A farmer conducts preliminary cleaning for freshly harvested durians at a durian orchard in Dak Lak province, Vietnam, on Sept. 15, 2023. Dak Lak is a leading durian-growing province in the country. As the vast majority of durians sold in the Chinese market are imported from Southeast Asia, the "king of fruits" has emerged as a prominent symbol of the booming China-ASEAN cooperation and China's vast market potential. (Photo by Pham Dinh Duc / Xinhua)

5·4·3

2023 年 9 月 15 日，在越南多樂省一家榴蓮加工廠，工人在給即將出口到中國的榴蓮貼牌。（新華社記者，胡佳麗攝）

Staff members label durians to be exported to China at a durian processing plant in Dak Lak province, Vietnam, on Sept. 15, 2023. (Xinhua / Hu Jiali)

5-4-4

2023 年 3 月 9 日，工人在緬甸仰光一家豆類加工廠檢查綠豆。（新華社稿，苗覺梭攝）

Workers check green grams at a beans and pulses processing plant in Yangon, Myanmar, March 9, 2023. (Photo by Myo Kyaw Soe / Xinhua)

5-4-5

2023 年 3 月 9 日，工人在緬甸仰光一家豆類加工廠搬運綠豆。搭乘〈區域全面經濟夥伴關係協定〉實施的東風，緬甸農產品出口向好。緬甸商務部表示，從 2022 年 4 月開始的 2022—2023 財年的近 11 個月裏，緬甸出口了超過 543,606 噸綠豆。（新華社稿，苗覺梭攝）

Workers carry bags of green grams at a beans and pulses processing plant in Yangon, Myanmar, March 9, 2023. Myanmar exported more than 543,606 tons of green grams in nearly 11 months of the 2022-2023 fiscal year beginning in April, 2022. (Photo by Myo Kyaw Soe / Xinhua)

5-5

松子、石榴和毛毯——阿富汗特產的進博會之旅

5-5-1

2018 年 11 月 12 日，在阿富汗東部霍斯特市，阿富汗農民準備出售松子。

阿富汗每年生產多達 2.3 萬噸松子，該國每年將通過空中走廊向中國出口價值 7 億至 8 億美元的松子。

在 2018 年上海中國國際進口博覽會上，阿富汗松子與當地特產一起出現在阿富汗展館，吸引大批參觀者。（新華社稿，扎曼· 扎里攝）

Afghan farmers prepare pine nut for sale in Khost city, eastern Afghanistan, on Nov. 12, 2018.

Up to 23,000 tons of pine nuts are produced each year in Afghanistan, the country will export between 700 million to 800 million U.S. dollars worth of pine nuts to China annually through the China-Afghanistan air corridor, Afghanistan displayed its pine nuts alongside many more local products in China International Import Expo (CIIE) in Shanghai in 2018.(Xinhua / Zaman Nazari)

5-5-2

2022 年 7 月 30 日，阿富汗喀布爾一家松子加工廠內，一名女工正在處理松子。（新華社稿，塞夫拉赫曼·薩菲攝）

Women work at a pine nut processing factory in Kabul, Afghanistan, July 30, 2022. (Photo by Saifurahman Safi / Xinhua)

5-5-3

2018 年 11 月 14 日，在阿富汗首都喀布爾，一名阿富汗男子在他的商店裏等待顧客。（新華社稿，拉赫马特·阿里扎达攝）

An Afghan man waits for customers at his shop in Kabul, capital of Afghanistan, Nov. 14, 2018. (Xinhua / Rahmat Alizadah)

5-5-4

2023 年 11 月 8 日，在阿富汗首都喀布爾，一名男子在展示地毯。（新華社稿，塞夫拉赫曼·薩菲攝）

A man displays a carpet in Kabul, Afghanistan, Nov. 8, 2023. (Photo by Saifurahman Safi / Xinhua)

5-5-5

2023 年 11 月 8 日，在阿富汗首都喀布爾，一名男子在編織地毯。

近年來，阿富汗製造的地毯已在多屆中國國際進口博覽會上展出，吸引大量客戶。阿富汗商人希望中國邀請更多的阿富汗企業家在國際博覽會上展出更多的產品。（新華社稿，塞夫拉赫曼·薩菲攝）

A man weaves a carpet in Kabul, Afghanistan, Nov. 8, 2023.

Afghan-made carpets have been put on display at several sessions of the China International Import Expo (CIIE) in recent years to attract clients. Afghan businesspeople want China to invite more Afghan entrepreneurs to put more products at the international fair. (Photo by Saifurahman Safi / Xinhua)

5-5-6

2023 年 11 月 4 日，在綠地全球商品貿易港內開設阿富汗國家進口館，阿里・法伊茲（左）和員工討論訂單設計。

阿富汗小夥阿里・法伊茲是參加過四屆進博會的"老朋友"。他 2014 年來中國學習中文時，發現在中國幾乎看不到阿富汗產品，了解到中國市場的潛力，決定努力把更多阿富汗產品推介給中國顧客。

2020 年，阿里和合夥人首次參加進博會，帶來了阿富汗手工地毯。他發現進博會提供了一個面向中國乃至世界推廣阿富汗商品的機會，於是連續四年赴約進博會。他的展位越來越大，帶來的產品越來越豐富。未來，他希望繼續拓展商品種類，將更多的阿富汗產品帶到中國市場。（新華社記者，王翔攝）

Ali Faiz (L) discusses the details of an order with an employee at the Greenland Global Commodity Trading Hub in east China's Shanghai, Nov. 4, 2023. It is the fourth time Faiz has participated in the expo since his first attendance in 2020 when he brought the handmade wool carpet, a specialty product of Afghanistan. The expo helped him obtain over 2,000 orders of carpets, which meant incomes for more than 2,000 local families for an entire year.

With his booth growing bigger and bigger and his exhibits becoming more and more diversified over these years in the expos, Faiz hopes to bring more Afghan products to China in the future. (Xinhua / Wang Xiang)

5-5-7

2023 年 11 月 6 日，在第六屆進博會食品及農產品展區，阿富汗食品吸引參展人員。（新華社記者，王翔攝）

Visitors are attracted by Afghan food and agricultural products at the 6th China International Import Expo (CIIE) in east China's Shanghai, Nov. 6, 2023. (Xinhua / Wang Xiang)

5-6

疫情催生數字化新經濟模式

5-6-1

2021 年 11 月 21 日，在馬來西亞彭亨州的勞勿，"Sam 貓山王榴蓮園" 園主梁沛鑫（中）與 Regaltech 總經理莊愷靖（左）和阿里雲工作人員曹國廷在榴蓮土壤傳感器旁交談。Regaltech 是一家位於馬來西亞首都吉隆坡的數字農業服務企業，專注於榴蓮數字種植服務，業務覆蓋馬來西亞和新加坡。2019 年，Regaltech 與阿里雲合作打造 "榴蓮雲平台"，在農場端通過智能傳感器收集農作物信息，並在雲上對土壤信息、肥料、天氣、樹木生長周期等進行分析，為榴蓮種植提供專業的指導方案。（新華社記者，朱煒攝）

Durian orchard owner Leong Pui Sam (C) talks with Alex Ch'ng (L), general manager of Regaltech, and Derick Choe with Alibaba Cloud, next to the sensor node at a durian orchard in Raub, Malaysia, Nov. 21, 2021.

Located in Kuala Lumpur, the capital city of Malaysia, Regaltech is a digital agritech service company which specializes in smart farming. In 2019, Regaltech collaborated with China's Alibaba Cloud in developing a cloud-based smart platform for durian plantation.

By collecting data through sensor nodes at the orchard and analyzing data such as Electric Conductivity, PH, soil moisture, weather, irrigation schedule on their cloud, the smart platform helps to provide professional guidance for durian farming. (Xinhua / Zhu Wei)

5-6-2

2020 年 4 月 25 日，在菲律賓帕西格市，一名裝扮成蜘蛛俠的男子向受 "強化社區隔離" 影響的滯留工人分發蔬菜。每次穿上蜘蛛俠服裝都自稱為 "蜘蛛俠丹" 的角色扮演者 Dan Geromo 裝扮成著名的超級英雄，一邊向因 "加強社區檢疫" 而無法回家與家人團聚的各省工人分發蔬菜，一邊為他們送去歡樂。疫情期間，菲律賓的電子平台外送業務逐漸興起。（新華社稿，烏馬利攝）

A man dressed as Spider-Man hands out bags of vegetables to a stranded worker affected by the "enhanced community quarantine" in Pasig City, the Philippines, on April 25, 2020. Cosplayer Dan Geromo, who calls himself "Spider-Dan" whenever he is wearing the Spider-Man costume, went out as the famous superhero to give joy while distributing vegetables to workers who are unable to go back home to their families in various provinces due to the enhanced community quarantine. During the COVID-19 pandemic, e-commerce delivery business picks up in the Philippines. (Photo by Rouelle Umali / Xinhua)

5-6-3

2022 年 9 月 19 日，參觀者在泰國曼谷舉行的 2022 華為全聯接大會上試用展品。在此間舉行的 2022 華為全聯接大會上，與會的東南亞各國專家認為有必要推動數字化進程，以確保經濟韌性和持續性復甦，並肯定中國方案對國家數字化轉型、人才培養等方面的貢獻。

為期三天的大會以"釋放數字生產力"為主題，邀請全球近萬名信息和通信技術（ICT）行業領袖、專家和合作夥伴等，共同探討釋放數字生產力、推動數字經濟、發展數字生態等議題。（新華社記者，林昊攝）

Visitors are seen at the Huawei Connect 2022 in Bangkok, Thailand, on Sept. 19, 2022.

Southeast Asian countries are looking at China's digital technology, as they are engaged in post-pandemic economic recovery and national digital transformation. (Xinhua / Lin Hao)

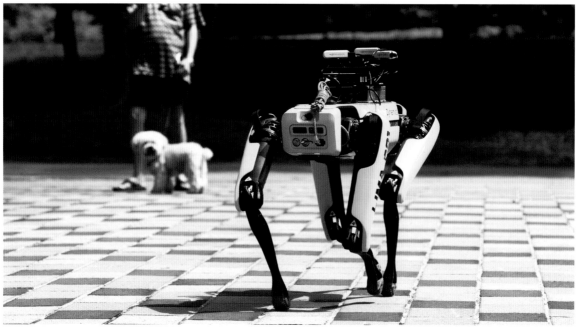

5-6-4

2020 年 9 月 22 日，一架由新加坡政府機構研發機器巡邏狗 SPOT 在新加坡碧山公園進行測訪客是否戴口罩或測試。這是新加坡採取的最新的防疫措施之一。這種由國家公園局、智慧國及數碼政府署與政府科技局攜手研發的自動巡邏機器狗 SPOT 除了有維持安全社交距離功能，也具有口罩檢測，視覺範圍之外的功能，無需激光雷達的 3D 映射和自主功能。（新華社稿，鄧智煒攝）

Robot dog SPOT which can detect whether visitors wear masks or not is seen during its second round trials in Singapore's Bishan Park, as part of measures against the spread of COVID-19, on Sept. 22, 2020. The four-legged robot is on its second round trials, jointly conducted by Singapore's National Parks Board (NParks) and the Smart Nation and Digital Government Group, and has increased capabilities like mask detection, beyond visual line of sight (BVLOS) and lidar-free 3D mapping. (Photo by Then Chih Wey / Xinhua)

5-6-5

2023 年 12 月 11 日，在印度尼西亞雅加達的丹那阿邦市場，一名商家通過 TikTok 電子商務服務上的直播推銷產品。（新華社稿，尤里法利攝）

A merchant promotes a product via live-streaming on the TikTok's e-commerce service at Tanah Abang Market in Jakarta, Indonesia, on Dec. 11, 2023. (Photo by Yorri Farli / Xinhua)

5-6-6

這是 2022 年 10 月 13 日拍攝的位於巴基斯坦卡拉奇市的自動化快遞分撥中心。由中國物流企業菜鳥物流與巴基斯坦電子商務公司達拉茲集團（Daraz Group）合作建設的自動化快遞分撥中心改變了過去巴基斯坦只能採用人工分揀快遞包裹的歷史。（新華社稿）

This photo taken on Oct. 13, 2022 shows an employee working at the smart distribution center in Karachi, Pakistan. (Xinhua)

5-7

日本匯率歷史最低

這是 2022 年 9 月 2 日在日本東京拍攝的顯示日元對美元匯率信息的電子顯示屏。受美聯儲宣佈加息 75 個基點，並預期加息或持續至明年消息影響，東京外匯市場日元對美元匯率 9 月 2 日一度跌破 140 日元兌 1 美元，創 24 年來新低。（新華社稿，龔岫熙攝）

A display shows an exchange rate between the Japanese yen and the U.S. dollar at a foreign exchange brokerage in Tokyo, Japan, on Sept. 2, 2022.

The Japanese government said the rapid decline of the yen could hurt both the economy and the stability of financial markets, as the Japanese currency tumbled to a fresh 24-year low against the U.S. dollar in the lower 140 yen range. (Photo by Gong Xiuxi / Xinhua)

5-8

通關後亞洲國家喜迎中國遊客回歸

5-8-1

2023 年 1 月 22 日，在印度尼西亞巴厘島巴厘島伍拉萊國際機場，中國小遊客在與一隻舞獅互動。印尼旅遊部和巴厘島省政府 22 日上午舉行儀式，歡迎 2023 年首個中國遊客包機從深圳抵達巴厘島。印尼方在巴厘島機場安排了當地傳統歌舞和極具中國春節特色的舞獅表演迎接中國遊客。機場為每名遊客獻上表示歡迎的花環，並贈送了紀念品。（新華社稿，比辛拉西攝）

Two Chinese child tourists with welcome wreaths interact with a lion dance performer at Bali Denpasar Ngurah Rai International Airport in Bali, Indonesia on Jan. 22, 2023. The Indonesian Ministry of Tourism and the Bali Provincial Government held a ceremony to welcome the first chartered flight of Chinese tourists from Shenzhen to Bali in 2023. (Photo by Dicky Bisinglasi / Xinhua)

5-8-2

2023 年 2 月 6 日，在泰國曼廊曼谷國際機場，一名中國遊客與工作人員自拍。當地時間 6 日上午 8 時左右，中國春秋航空公司一架由廣州起飛的客機降落在泰國首都曼谷廊曼國際機場，這是在中國試點恢復出境團隊旅遊業務首日，泰國迎來的首批中國團隊遊客。當標誌性的“團旗”出現在旅客到達出口時，熱烈的掌聲在大廳裏響起。在此等候的泰國國家旅遊局局長育他沙迎上前，向中國遊客送上花環和禮品，並用中文說：“歡迎光臨！”（新華社記者，王騰攝）

A Chinese tourist takes a selfie with Thai staff members at Don Mueang International Airport in Bangkok, Thailand, Feb. 6, 2023. Three years after the pandemic, the first tour groups from China arrived in the Thai capital of Bangkok, greeted by flowers and a warm welcome from the Southeast Asian country betting on tourists' return to boost the recovery of its vital tourism sector. (Xinhua / Wang Teng)

5-8-3

2023 年 9 月 25 日，泰國總理賽塔·他威信（前，右）在素萬那普國際機場迎接中國遊客。自 9 月 25 日起，泰國對中國遊客實施為期約 5 個月的免簽政策。當天上午，賽塔·他威信與多名政府高官前往首都曼谷的素萬那普國際機場迎接中國遊客。（新華社稿，拉亨攝）

Thai Prime Minister Srettha Thavisin (R, front) welcomes Chinese tourists at Suvarnabhumi airport in Bangkok, Thailand, Sept. 25, 2023. Thailand extended a warm welcome to the first batch of visa-exempt flights from China, marking the launch of the nation's fresh initiative to reinvigorate its Chinese tourist market. (Photo by Rachen Sageamsak / Xinhua)

5-8-4

2023 年 2 月 7 日，柬埔寨旅遊大臣童昆（中）在金邊國際機場為中國旅客帶上該國傳統的高棉圍巾。當天，一架載有中國乘客的國航航班抵達柬埔寨首都金邊國際機場，受到柬埔寨旅遊大臣童昆和中國駐柬埔寨大使王文天等的熱烈歡迎。柬埔寨旅遊資源豐富，既有聞名於世的吳哥窟等世界文化遺產，也有洞里薩湖等自然風光。自 2023 年 2 月 6 日起，中國試點恢復赴柬埔寨等 20 個國家的出境團隊旅遊和"機票＋酒店"業務。柬旅遊部表示，熱烈歡迎中國遊客的到來並已做好充分準備。（新華社稿，批隆攝）

Cambodian Tourism Minister Thong Khon (C) presents traditional scarf to a Chinese tourist at the Phnom Penh International Airport on Feb. 7, 2023. A flight carrying some 140 Chinese tourists in a tour group landed at the airport, receiving a warm welcome from Cambodian tourism officials and tour operators. It was the first group tour of Chinese tourists to the country after a three-year hiatus due to the COVID-19 pandemic. China was the largest source of foreign tourists to Cambodia in the pre-pandemic era, according to the country's Tourism Ministry. (Photo by Phearum / Xinhua)

5-9

東方之珠依然璀璨

5-9-1

2022 年 7 月 1 日，香港特區政府在金紫荊廣場舉行升旗儀式，慶祝香港回歸祖國 25 週年。這是分別懸掛中華人民共和國國旗、香港特區區旗的直升機從空中飛過。（新華社記者，盧炳輝攝）

Helicopters carrying China's national flag and the flag of the Hong Kong Special Administrative Region fly over Hong Kong, south China, July 1, 2022. A flag-raising ceremony was held by the government of the Hong Kong Special Administrative Region to celebrate the 25th anniversary of Hong Kong's return to the motherland. (Xinhua / Lo Ping Fai)

5-9-2

這是 2023 年 5 月 27 日在香港長洲島拍攝的"搶包山"比賽現場。伴隨著整齊劃一的倒數呼喊聲，銅鑼被敲響，香港長洲太平清醮的重頭戲"搶包山"決賽於 5 月 27 日零時整開始，9 男 3 女共 12 位選手隨即飛奔攀上約 14 米高的仿真包山。時隔 3 年，香港這一獨有的傳統文化盛事再現，成千上萬香港市民及遊客慕名前來一睹盛況。（新華社記者，李鋼攝）

People watch a bun scrambling competition during the annual Bun Festival in Cheung Chau, a small island south of Hong Kong, south China, May 27, 2023. The Bun Festival, one of Hong Kong's most colorful cultural celebration events, has been on China's national list of intangible cultural heritage since 2011. (Xinhua / Li Gang)

5-9-3

2023 年 9 月 28 日，人們在香港參加有著百餘年歷史的香港傳統民俗活動 "大坑舞火龍"。火龍穿越大街小巷，與市民共迎中秋。當晚 20 時 15 分許，火龍開始在一片歡快的鑼鼓聲中沿著傳統路綫巡遊舞動，平日寧靜的街道一時間火光閃爍。(新華社記者，朱煒攝)

Photo taken on Sept. 28, 2023 shows the "Fire Dragon Dance" performed on a street on the eve of the Mid-Autumn Festival, in Tai Hang of Hong Kong, south China. In 2011, Tai Hang fire dragon dance was listed as China's official intangible cultural heritage. (Xinhua / Zhu Wei)

5-9-4

2020 年 6 月 11 日，網易正式在香港交易所掛牌上市。網易在港交所採取 "雲敲鑼" 的網絡上市儀式，以在杭州進行的網絡視頻形式替代現場上市儀式。(新華社稿)

A ceremony is held to celebrate the debut of NetEase Inc.'s shares on Hong Kong Exchanges and Clearing Limited (HKEX) in Hangzhou, capital of east China's Zhejiang Province, June 11, 2020. (Xinhua)

5-10

亞洲發展中國家的農業現代化進程

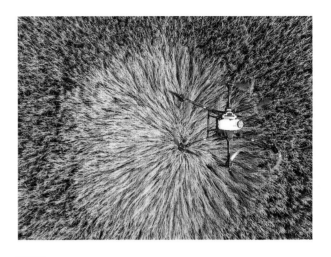

5-10-1

這是 2023 年 11 月 12 日在孟加拉國諾爾辛迪拍攝的化肥廠項目。當日，由中企參與承建的孟加拉國古拉紹—布拉什化肥廠舉行項目落成儀式，成為該國首個可回收利用二氧化碳的綠色化肥廠。孟加拉國總理謝赫·哈西娜在儀式致辭時表示，項目將使該國尿素產量增加 10%，減少化肥進口量，創造更多就業機會。（新華社稿，吉本攝）

This photo taken on Nov. 12, 2023 shows the Ghorashal-Polash Urea Fertilizer Project in Narsingdi, Bangladesh. Bangladeshi Prime Minister Sheikh Hasina has inaugurated the South Asian country's largest and first-ever green fertilizer factory. Construction of the project started in 2020, and the China National Chemical Engineering & Construction Corporation Seven Ltd. (CC7), in collaboration with its Japanese partner Mitsubishi Heavy Industries (MHI), had been striving for the mega project to be completed as scheduled. (Photo by Jibon Ahsan / Xinhua)

5-10-2

2022 年 8 月 1 日，大疆農業植保無人機在泰國黎逸府噴灑農藥（無人機拍攝）。近年來，以植保無人機為代表的智能化機械在農業生產中大顯身手。中國製造的農業植保無人機為泰國當地農民賦能，推動農業生產更加高效安全。（新華社記者，王騰攝）

Aerial photo taken on Aug. 1, 2022 shows a DJI agricultural drone spraying pesticides in Roi Et, Thailand. China-made agricultural drones are seen flying over grain fields in this southeast Asian country to help local farmers produce more efficiently, conveniently and safely. (Xinhua / Wang Teng)

5-10-3

這是 2023 年 2 月 11 日在阿富汗帕爾萬省拍攝的部分水利工程。阿富汗的兩條主要河流潘傑希爾河和戈爾班德河均流經帕爾萬省，但該省曾經因缺乏水利基礎設施導致當地農田缺少灌溉用水，大片土地荒蕪。中國政府於 20 世紀六七十年代援建了帕爾萬水利灌溉工程，可灌溉當地數萬公頃土地，同時也可供應人畜飲水和生活用水。工程對阿富汗經濟發展起著重要作用，經濟效益顯著，因而在阿富汗家喻戶曉，人們深情地稱之為"生命之水工程"。（新華社稿，塞夫拉赫曼·薩菲攝）

This photo taken on Feb. 11, 2023 shows parts of a water canal project in Afghanistan's Parwan Province. Although located near Afghanistan's longest rivers, the province once suffered from drought and thus large swathes of land were left uncultivated due to the lack of irrigation systems. A water canal project in Parwan, built by China and provided as aid to Afghanistan, was put into use in the 1970s. Irrigating thousands of hectares of farmland, the Chinese-initiated project is described as vital for the development of Parwan's agricultural sector. (Photo by Saifurahman Safi / Xinhua)

5-11

中國助力南太國家發展菌草技術

2018 年 6 月 12 日，在斐濟楠迪，中國專家和當地僱員檢查菌菇生長情況。助力中國治理荒漠化的"利器"——菌草易於種植，以菌草技術栽培食用菇、藥用菌，製作粗蛋白含量高、產量大的飼料，是致富的有效途徑。自引入以來，菌草技術在斐濟扎根、開花、結果，有力促進了該國農業的可持續發展，被當地民眾稱為助力斐濟減貧致富的"幸福草"。（新華社記者，張永興攝）

This photo taken on June 12, 2018 shows an Chinese expert and local employees checking mushroom cultivation in Nadi, Fiji's third largest city. Juncao, a type of special grass that could be used to cultivate edible and medicinal mushrooms and feed livestock, has been bringing tangible benefits to Fijians. (Xinhua / Zhang Yongxing)

2018 年 6 月 12 日，在斐濟楠迪，中國專家和當地僱員檢查菌菇生長情況。菌草統指可作為栽培食用和藥用菌培養基的草本植物。菌類一般都生長在成段樹木或木屑中，上世紀八十年代，中國福建農林大學的林佔熺教授成功開發出"以草代木"栽培食藥用菌的技術。此後，菌草不僅在中國的乾旱荒漠化地區種植，更向斐濟、盧旺達、萊索托等多國推廣，助力當地發展。（新華社記者，張永興攝）

This photo taken on June 12, 2018 shows an Chinese expert and local employees checking mushroom cultivation in Nadi, Fiji's third largest city. The Juncao technology (Jun means fungi and Cao means grass) was invented in the 1980s by Lin Zhanxi, a professor at China's Fujian Agriculture and Forestry University, who is also the chief scientist for the China-Fiji Juncao Technology Cooperation Project which was established in 2014 after the Chinese and Fijian governments inked an agreement to start the agriculture cooperation. (Xinhua / Zhang Yongxing)

2020 年 12 月 15 日，林應興（戴草帽者）在巴布亞新幾內亞東高地省中國援助巴新菌草和旱稻技術項目第 9 期培訓班上授課。林應興是中國援巴布亞新幾內亞菌草旱稻項目專家組組長。他和同事們負責為東高地省亨加諾菲區一個基層社區的 117 名農民進行菌草和旱稻種植技術培訓。為了讓學員對菌草旱稻的收益有一個更直觀的認識，他們準備了 50 多公斤旱稻米和 10 公斤用菌草培育的新鮮蘑菇，讓學員們在午餐時品嚐。（新華社稿）

Lin Yingxing (with hat), specialist from the Fujian Agriculture and Forestry University, gives lecture in the field to local residents in the Eastern Highlands Province of Papua New Guinea, on Dec. 15, 2020. The Juncao and upland rice farming technologies are listed as priorities under the Eastern Highlands five-year plan to help local communities eradicate poverty, ensure food security and achieve sustainable development. (Xinhua)

2020 年 12 月 17 日，在巴布亞新幾內亞東高地省，參加中國援助巴新菌草和旱稻技術項目第 9 期培訓班的當地民眾展示結業證書。1997 年，應巴新東高地省政府邀請，福建農林大學研究員林佔熺帶領團隊在當地建立了菌草技術示範點。在巴布亞新幾內亞，菌草被稱作"林草"，以表達對中國扶貧專家的感激。（新華社稿）

Residents display their certificates of training courses on Juncao and upland rice cultivation technology in the Eastern Highlands Province of Papua New Guinea, Dec. 17, 2020. The cooperation on fungi and rice cultivation between China and PNG dates back two decades ago, and has yielded fruitful results. (Xinhua)

亞太地區的世界文化和非物質文化遺產非常豐富，其中大部分為聯合國教科文組織認定的世界遺產。本組相冊從攝影美學的角度，選取了這些世界遺產的精彩瞬間，展現了各民族智慧的結晶和全人類文明的瑰寶。

The Asia-Pacific region boasts a rich tangible and intangible cultural heritage, with a significant portion recognized by the United Nations Educational, Scientific and Cultural Organization (UNESCO) as world heritage. This section of the album, from the perspective of photographic aesthetics, captures the splendid moments of these world heritage sites, showcasing the crystallization of the wisdom of countries across the Asia-Pacific and the treasures of human civilization.

6

文化遺產
Tangible and Intangible Cultural Heritage

6-1

緬甸仰光大金塔

6-1-1

2020 年 11 月 29 日的緬甸仰光，一輪滿月升起在仰光大金塔上。仰光大金塔是緬甸最神聖的佛塔，也是緬甸最寶貴的文化遺產之一，代表著建築、雕塑和藝術的精髓。（新華社稿，吳昂攝）

A full moon rises above the Shwedagon Pagoda in Yangon, Myanmar, Nov. 29, 2020. Shwedagon Pagoda is the most sacred Buddhist pagoda in Myanmar. It is a repository of one of Myanmar's best heritages, representing architecture, sculpture and arts. (Photo by U Aung / Xinhua)

6-1-2

2022 年 9 月 1 日傍晚晚霞映襯下的緬甸仰光大金塔。（新華社稿，苗覺梭攝）

Photo taken on Sept. 1, 2022 shows the sunset behind Shwedagon Pagoda in Yangon, Myanmar. (Photo by Myo Kyaw Soe / Xinhua)

6-2

吳哥考古公園

6-2-1

2021 年 5 月 24 日，柬埔寨暹粒市的吳哥考古公園。吳哥考古公園位於暹粒省，於 1992 年被列入聯合國教科文組織世界遺產名錄，是該國最受歡迎的旅遊勝地。（新華社稿，柬埔寨吳哥古跡保護和管理機構供圖）

Photo taken on May 24, 2021 shows a view of the Angkor Archaeological Park in Siem Reap, Cambodia. Located in Siem Reap province, the Angkor Archeological Park, inscribed on the World Heritage List of the UNESCO in 1992, is the kingdom's most popular tourist destination. (Apsara National Authority / Handout via Xinhua)

6-2-2

2021 年 5 月 21 日，柬埔寨暹粒市的吳哥考古公園。（新華社稿，柬埔寨吳哥古跡保護和管理機構供圖）

Photo taken on May 21, 2021 shows a view of the Angkor Archaeological Park in Siem Reap, Cambodia. (Apsara National Authority / Handout via Xinhua)

6-3

巴基斯坦巴爾蒂特堡

6-3-1

2020 年 10 月 17 日拍攝的照片顯示巴基斯坦北部吉爾吉特－巴爾蒂斯坦地區罕薩山谷的舊城中巴爾蒂特堡的景色。創立於公元 8 世紀的巴爾蒂特堡是巴基斯坦著名的歷史遺跡，自 2004 年起被列入聯合國教科文組織世界遺產預備名錄。（新華社稿，艾哈邁德·卡瑪爾攝）

Photo taken on Oct. 17, 2020 shows a view of Baltit Fort in the old city of Hunza valley in Pakistan's northern Gilgit-Baltistan region. Founded in the 8th century CE, Baltit Fort is a prominent historical site in Pakistan. It has been on the UNESCO World Heritage Tentative list since 2004. (Photo by Ahmad Kamal / Xinhua)

2020 年 10 月 17 日拍攝的照片顯示巴基斯坦北部吉爾吉特－巴爾蒂斯坦地區罕薩山谷的舊城中巴爾蒂特堡的景色。（新華社記者，劉天攝）

Photo taken on Oct. 17, 2020 shows a view of Baltit Fort in the old city of Hunza valley in Pakistan's northern Gilgit-Baltistan region. (Xinhua / Liu Tian)

6-4

印度顧特卜塔

6-4-1

2020 年 2 月 13 日，遊客參觀印度首都新德里的顧特卜塔。顧特卜塔為聯合國教科文組織認定的世界文化遺產，它位於德里南部幾公里處，建於 13 世紀早期。這座紅砂石尖塔高 72.5 米。基座直徑 14.32 米，塔峰直徑 2.75 米。（新華社稿，賈維德·達爾攝）

People visit the Qutub Minar, a UNESCO World Heritage site, in New Delhi, India, Feb. 13, 2020. Built in the early 13th century a few kilometers south of Delhi, the red sandstone tower of Qutb Minar is 72.5m high, tapering from 2.75m in diameter at its peak to 14.32m at its base. (Photo by Javed Dar / Xinhua)

6-4-2

2020 年 2 月 13 日，一架飛機飛越
印度首都新德里的顧特卜塔。（新
華社稿，賈維德・達爾攝）

An airplane flies near Qutub Minar, a
UNESCO World Heritage site, in New
Delhi, India, Feb. 13, 2020. (Photo by
Javed Dar / Xinhua)

6-5

老撾琅勃拉邦古城

6-5-1

2020 年 1 月 1 日，湄公河畔的老撾琅勃拉邦古城的日落風光。位於老撾北部的琅勃拉邦古城於 1995 年被聯合國教科文組織列為世界文化遺產。琅勃拉邦古城是老撾傳統建築和城市結構與 19 世紀至 20 世紀歐洲殖民建築相融合的突出典範。（新華社稿，凱喬攝）

Photo taken on Jan. 1, 2020 shows the sunset scenery of Luang Prabang town on the riverside of Mekong River in Laos. Located in northern Laos, Luang Prabang was listed by the UNESCO as a world heritage in 1995. It is an outstanding example of the fusion of Lao traditional architecture and urban structures with those built by the European colonial authorities in the 19th and 20th centuries. (Photo by Kaikeo Saiyasane / Xinhua)

6-5-2

2020 年 1 月 2 日，湄公河畔的老撾琅
勃拉邦古城的日出風光。（新華社稿，
凱喬攝）

Photo taken on Jan. 2, 2020 shows the
sunrise scenery of Luang Prabang town on
the riverside of Mekong River, Laos. (Photo
by Kaikeo Saiyasane / Xinhua)

6-6

澳大利亞悉尼歌劇院

6-6

2023 年 10 月 20 日晚，澳大利亞悉尼歌劇院被彩燈照亮，以慶祝其50 歲生日。自 1973 年竣工以來，這個澳大利亞地標吸引了數百萬遊客，並於 2007 年被聯合國教科文組織列為世界文化遺產。（新華社稿，胡涇辰攝）

Sydney Opera House is lit up for its 50th birthday in Sydney, Australia, Oct. 20, 2023. Since its completion in 1973, the iconic Australian landmark has attracted millions of visitors and in 2007 became a UNESCO World Heritage site. (Photo by Hu Jingchen / Xinhua)

6-7

斯里蘭卡平納維拉大象孤兒院

6-7-1 & 6-7-2

2023 年 6 月 26 日，在斯里蘭卡平納維拉，大象孤兒院的大象在河水中洗澡。斯里蘭卡平納維拉大象孤兒院建於 1975 年，是世界上第一個為大象建立的孤兒院。（新華社稿，阿吉特·佩雷拉攝）

Elephants bathe in a river at the Pinnawala Elephant Orphanage, Sri Lanka, June 26, 2023. Established in 1975, the Pinnawala Elephant Orphanage is the world's first orphanage dedicated to elephants. (Photo by Ajith Perera / Xinhua)

6-8

泰國曼谷大皇宮

6-8-1

2023 年 5 月 1 日中國遊客參觀泰國曼谷大皇宮景區。大皇宮建築群建於 1782 年，不僅包括皇家和王座大廳，還包括一些政府辦公室，以及著名的玉佛寺。（新華社記者，王騰攝）

Chinese tourists visit the Grand Palace scenic spot in Bangkok, Thailand, May 1, 2023. Established in 1782, the Grand Palace complex consists of not only royal and throne halls, but also a number of government offices as well as the renowned Temple of the Emerald Buddha. (Xinhua / Wang Teng)

6-8-2

2023 年 6 月 15 日遊客在泰國曼谷大皇宮景區拍照。（新華社記者，王騰攝）

Tourists take photos at the Grand Palace scenic spot in Bangkok, Thailand, June 15, 2023. (Xinhua / Wang Teng)

6-9

尼泊爾巴克塔普爾王宮廣場

6-9-1 & 6-9-2

2021 年 7 月 11 日，位於尼泊爾巴克塔普爾王宮廣場的尼亞塔波拉神廟。巴克塔普爾王宮廣場展示了尼泊爾的古老建築、藝術和文化，於 1979 年被列為聯合國教科文組織世界文化遺產。（新華社稿，蘇拉韋·什雷斯塔攝）

Photo shows the Nyatapola temple at Bhaktapur Durbar Square in Bhaktapur, Nepal, July 11, 2021. The Bhaktapur Durbar Square, which features ancient architectures, arts and culture of Nepal, was listed as a UNESCO world heritage site in 1979. (Photo by Sulav Shrestha / Xinhua)

6-10

日本鎌倉市

6-10-1

這是 2020 年 8 月 27 日在日本鎌倉拍攝的高德院內的鎌倉大佛。鎌倉位於日本神奈川縣，其三面環山一面臨海，是一座兼具自然之美與歷史文化氣息的古都。（新華社記者，杜瀟逸攝）

Photo taken on Aug. 27, 2020 shows the Kamakura Daibutsu (The Great Buddha of Kamakura) at Kotoku-in Temple in Kamakura, Japan. Kamakura is a city in Kanagawa Prefecture, Japan. Surrounded by mountains on three sides and facing the sea on one side, Kamakura boasts a harmonious blend of nature beauty and historical culture. (Xinhua / Du Xiaoyi)

6-10-2

這是 2020 年 8 月 27 日在日本鎌倉拍攝的鶴岡八幡宮。（新華社記者，杜瀟逸攝）

Photo taken on Aug. 27, 2020 shows a view of Tsurugaoka Hachimangu Shrine in Kamakura, Japan. (Xinhua / Du Xiaoyi)

6-11

韓國昌德宮

6-11-2

2019 年 5 月 21 日，韓國首爾的昌德宮後苑內一景。（新華社記者，王婧嬙攝）

Photo taken on May 21, 2019 shows the Changdeokgung Palace in Seoul, South Korea. (Xinhua / Wang Jingqiang)

6-11-1

2019 年 5 月 21 日，身著傳統韓服的遊客在韓國首爾的昌德宮後苑內遊覽。昌德宮於 1997 年被聯合國教科文組織列為世界文化遺產，其建築風格很好體現了自然和建築物的和諧統一。（新華社記者，王婧嬙攝）

People dressed in traditional Korean clothing visit the Changdeokgung Palace in Seoul, South Korea, May 21, 2019. Changdeokgung Palace was listed as a UNESCO world heritage site in 1997 and is regarded as a masterpiece of architecture as the buildings are in harmony with the natural settings. (Xinhua / Wang Jingqiang)

6-12

越南傳統服飾奧黛

6-12-1 & 6-12-2

2018 年 3 月 4 日，在越南胡志明市奧黛文化節開幕式上，模特們身著奧黛走秀。奧黛（長襖）是越南的傳統民族服裝，通常由絲綢或其他柔軟的面料製成，是越南女性在特殊場合最受歡迎的服裝。（新華社稿，黃氏香攝）

Models wearing Ao Dai perform during Ao Dai Festival 2018 in Ho Chi Minh City, Vietnam, on March 4, 2018. Ao Dai (Long Dress), a Vietnamese traditional costume normally made of silk or other soft fabrics, is the most popular dress by Vietnamese women on special occasions. (Photo by Hoang Thi Huong / Xinhua)

6-13

印尼菲尼斯帆船

6-13-1 & 6-13-2

2023 年 6 月 1 日，一名工作人員在印度尼西亞中爪哇省克拉登的一間工作室內製作迷你菲尼斯帆船。菲尼斯帆船是一種由木材製成的印尼傳統標誌性船隻，起源於南蘇拉威西省，於 2017 年被列入聯合國教科文組織人類非物質文化遺產代表作名錄。（新華社稿，布拉姆·塞洛攝）

A worker makes a miniature Pinisi ship at a workshop in Klaten, Central Java, Indonesia, on June 1, 2023. Pinisi is an iconic Indonesian traditional boat made of wood, which originates from South Sulawesi province. It was inscribed on the Representative List of the Intangible Cultural Heritage of Humanity in 2017. (Photo by Bram Selo / Xinhua)

6-14

新加坡小販文化

6-14-1 & 6-14-2

2020 年 12 月 17 日，食客在新加坡竹腳小販中心用餐。新加坡的小販文化於 2020 年被列入聯合國教科文組織人類非物質文化遺產代表作名錄。起源於街頭美食文化的小販中心已成為新加坡這個多元文化城邦國家的標誌。小販從多元文化的融合中汲取靈感，改良菜餚以適應本地口味和需求。如今，新加坡各地的小販中心繼續在居住區、休閒區和工作區為多元化社區提供服務。（新華社稿，鄧智煒攝）

People have their meals at Singapore's Tekka hawker center on Dec. 17, 2020. Singapore's hawker culture was inscribed on the UNESCO Representative List of the Intangible Cultural Heritage of Humanity in 2020. Evolved from street food culture, hawker centers have become markers of Singapore as a multicultural city-state. Hawkers take inspiration from the confluence of these cultures, adapting dishes to local tastes and contexts. Today, hawker centers across Singapore continue serving the needs of diverse communities in residential, recreational and work districts. (Photo by Then Chih Wey / Xinhua)

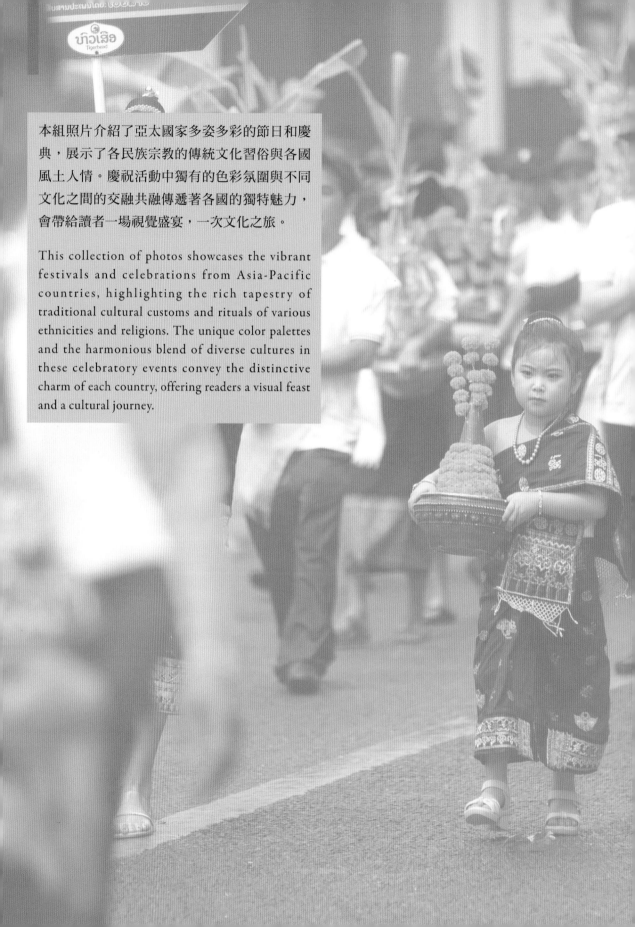

本組照片介紹了亞太國家多姿多彩的節日和慶典，展示了各民族宗教的傳統文化習俗與各國風土人情。慶祝活動中獨有的色彩氛圍與不同文化之間的交融共融傳遞著各國的獨特魅力，會帶給讀者一場視覺盛宴，一次文化之旅。

This collection of photos showcases the vibrant festivals and celebrations from Asia-Pacific countries, highlighting the rich tapestry of traditional cultural customs and rituals of various ethnicities and religions. The unique color palettes and the harmonious blend of diverse cultures in these celebratory events convey the distinctive charm of each country, offering readers a visual feast and a cultural journey.

7

多彩節慶
Vibrant Festivals

7-1

一年伊始──新年

每年的 1 月 1 日，世界各國人民歡聚一堂，慶祝新一年的到來，寄託對美好未來的期望，回顧過去一年的收穫與成長。

On Jan. 1 every year, people around the world come together to celebrate the arrival of the new year, expressing hopes for a bright future and reflecting on the achievements and growth of the past year.

7-1-1

2024 年 1 月 1 日，澳大利亞悉尼燃放煙花迎接新年。辭舊迎新之際，人們在世界各地迎接新的一年。（新華社記者，梁有昶攝）

Fireworks are set off to celebrate the New Year in Sydney, Australia, Jan. 1, 2024. (Xinhua / Liang Youchang)

7-1-2

2023 年 12 月 30 日，在巴基斯坦伊斯蘭堡，人們在一處 "2024" 字樣的裝飾彩燈前拍照。2024 年即將到來，多地迎新年氣氛漸濃。（新華社稿，艾哈邁德·卡邁勒攝）

People take photos in front of a light installation for the New Year in Islamabad, Pakistan, Dec. 30, 2023. (Photo by Ahmad Kamal / Xinhua)

7-1-3

2023 年 12 月 31 日晚，新年焰火在印度尼西亞日惹的巴蘭班南神廟上空綻放。世界各地民眾送別 2023，慶祝新年的到來。（新華社稿，阿貢·蘇普里揚托攝）

Fireworks are set off during New Year's Eve celebration at Prambanan Temple in Yogyakarta, Indonesia, Dec. 31, 2023. (Photo by Agung Supriyanto / Xinhua)

7-1-4

2024 年 1 月 1 日凌晨，煙花在香港維多利亞港上空綻放。當日，香港舉行煙花匯演，迎接 2024 的到來。（新華社記者，朱煒攝）

Fireworks in celebration of the New Year illuminate the sky over Victoria Harbor in Hong Kong, south China, Jan. 1, 2024. (Xinhua / Zhu Wei)

7-2

百節年為首，四季春為先 —— 春節

農曆春節，又稱中國傳統新年，是中國最重要的傳統節日之一。家人團聚、共享美食、賞花燈是春節的傳統活動。此外，亞洲地區的許多國家如越南、馬來西亞、新加坡等也慶祝農曆春節。

The Lunar New Year, also known as the Chinese Spring Festival, is one of China's most important traditional celebrations. Marked by family reunions, festive feasts, and lantern displays, it symbolizes new beginnings. Additionally, many Asian countries including Vietnam, Malaysia, Singapore also celebrate the Lunar New Year.

7-2-1

2022 年 1 月 23 日，人們在馬來西亞吉隆坡一家市場選購新年裝飾。隨著農曆新年的臨近，馬來西亞本地華人紛紛購買新年裝飾，迎接春節到來。（新華社記者，朱煒攝）

People buy decorations for Chinese New Year at a store in Kuala Lumpur, Malaysia, Jan. 23, 2022. People decorate their houses with plants and flowers as well as traditional decorations such as red lanterns and couplets as the Chinese New Year draws closer. (Xinhua / Zhu Wei)

7-2-2

2023 年 1 月 22 日零時許，馬來西亞吉隆坡的天后宮燃放煙花，慶祝新春佳節。（新華社稿，張紋綜攝）

Fireworks illuminate the sky over the Thean Hou Temple in Kuala Lumpur, Malaysia in celebration of the Chinese New Year, Jan. 22, 2023. (Photo by Chong Voon Chung / Xinhua)

7-2-3

2022 年 1 月 31 日，日本東京的地標性建築東京塔點亮 "中國紅"，慶祝中國農曆新年。（新華社記者，張笑宇攝）

Tokyo Tower is lit up in Chinese red to celebrate the Chinese Lunar New Year, in Tokyo, Japan, Jan. 31, 2022. (Xinhua / Zhang Xiaoyu)

7-2-4

2023 年 1 月 22 日，菲律賓馬尼拉舉辦龍舟賽活動，慶祝農曆新年的到來。（新華社稿，烏馬利攝）

Rowing teams participate in a dragon boat race along Pasig River to celebrate the Chinese New Year in Manila, the Philippines, Jan. 22, 2023. (Photo by Rouelle Umali / Xinhua)

7-2-5

2023 年 2 月 4 日，澳大利亞悉尼達令港舉行水上舞獅表演，慶祝中國農曆新年及元宵節。（新華社記者，白雪飛攝）

People using water jetpacks perform lion dance to celebrate the Chinese New Year and the Lantern Festival at Darling Harbour in Sydney, Australia, Feb. 4, 2023. (Xinhua / Bai Xuefei)

7-3

印度傳統新年——灑紅節

每年印度曆 12 月（公曆 2 月底或 3 月初）的月圓夜是灑紅節的開始。這個節日是印度的狂歡節，意味著冬季的結束和春季的來臨。無論在城鎮還是鄉村，人們都會跑到街道上，或到親朋好友家，或聚集在公共場所，互相潑灑提前準備好的彩粉或彩水。人身上的色彩越多，表明得到的福氣就越多。泰國、斯里蘭卡、菲律賓等國也慶祝灑紅節。

Every year, on the full moon night of the 12th month in the Indian calendar (usually late February or early March), the Holi festival begins in India. This celebration marks the end of winter and the arrival of spring. People both in urban and rural areas take to the streets, visit friends and family, and gather in public spaces to playfully splash each other with colored powders or colored water. The more colors one has on them, the more blessings they are believed to receive. Holi is celebrated by Hindu residents around the world, including in Thailand, Sri Lanka, the Philippines, etc.

7-3-1
2023 年 3 月 8 日，一名男子在印度新德里參加灑紅節慶祝活動。（新華社稿，賈韋德·達爾攝）

A man is smeared with colored powder during a celebration of the Holi festival in New Delhi, India, March 8, 2023. (Photo by Javed Dar / Xinhua)

7-3-2

2023 年 3 月 11 日，人們在泰國芭堤雅參加灑紅節慶祝活動。（新華社稿，拉亨攝）

People play with colored powder to celebrate the Holi festival in Pattaya, Thailand, March 11, 2023. (Photo by Rachen Sageamsak / Xinhua)

7-3-3

2023 年 3 月 12 日，人們在斯里蘭卡卡圖納耶克參加灑紅節慶祝活動。（新華社稿，阿吉特・佩雷拉攝）

People smeared with colored powder take part in a celebration of the Holi festival in Katunayake, Sri Lanka, March 12, 2023. (Photo by Ajith Perera / Xinhua)

7-3-4

2023 年 3 月 11 日，人們在菲律賓帕賽參加灑紅節慶祝活動。（新華社稿，烏馬利攝）

People take part in the celebration during the Holi Festival in Pasay City, the Philippines, March 11, 2023. The Hindu festival Holi, also known as the "Festival of Colors," is celebrated by Hindu residents around the world. (Photo by Rouelle Umali / Xinhua)

7-4

泰國盛大潑水節日——宋干節

潑水節也稱宋干節，是老撾、泰國的傳統新年節日，人們會以互相潑水的方式表達迎新祝福。

Celebrated in April, the Songkran Festival, or the Lao/Thai New Year is the most important festival in the two countries and also a time of endless fun for the people. People express greetings by splashing water on each other.

7-4-1
2023 年 4 月 13 日，人們在泰國曼谷慶祝潑水節。（新華社稿，拉亨攝）

People attend water fight to celebrate the Songkran Festival in Bangkok, Thailand, April 13, 2023. (Photo by Rachen Sageamsak / Xinhua)

2023 年 4 月 13 日，泰國廊開的民眾慶祝潑水節。（新華社記者，林昊攝）

Locals celebrate the Songkran festival in Nong Khai province, Thailand, April 13, 2023. (Xinhua / Lin Hao)

2023 年 4 月 14 日，人們在老撾首都萬象街頭參加潑水節慶祝活動。潑水節也稱宋干節，是老撾的傳統新年節日，慶祝方式多樣。（新華社稿，凱喬攝）

People participate in a street activity celebrating the Songkran festival in Vientiane, Laos, April 14, 2023. The Songkran is a Lao traditional New Year's festival celebrated in multiple ways. (Photo by Kaikeo Saiyasane / Xinhua)

7-4-4

2023 年 4 月 16 日，孩子們在老撾琅勃拉邦參加潑水節活動。（新華社稿，凱喬攝）

Children participate in the celebration of the Songkran Festival in Luang Prabang, Laos, April 16, 2023. (Photo by Kaikeo Saiyasane / Xinhua)

7-5

佛陀紀念日——衛塞節

衛塞節是為慶祝佛陀降生、成道、涅槃
"三期同一慶"的節日。

Vesak Day is a festival celebrated to
commemorate the triple events of
the Buddha's birth, enlightenment,
and nirvana, known as the "Threefold
Blessing" in honor of these significant
milestones in his life.

7-5-1

2023 年 5 月 5 日，佛教徒在斯里蘭卡科倫坡市郊一
處寺廟參加衛塞節慶祝活動。（新華社稿，阿吉特·
佩雷拉攝）

Buddhists are seen in a temple in the outskirts of Colombo,
Sri Lanka, May 5, 2023. (Photo by Ajith Perera / Xinhua)

7-5-2
2023 年 6 月 4 日，人們在印度尼西亞馬格朗的衛塞節慶祝活動上放飛燈籠。（新華社稿，阿貢‧蘇普里揚托攝）

People release sky lanterns during the Vesak Day celebration at Borobudur temple in Magelang, Central Java, Indonesia, on June 4, 2023. (Photo by Agung Supriyantoo / Xinhua)

7-6

伊斯蘭齋月結束 —— 開齋節

開齋節，是伊斯蘭教最重要的節日之一。這一節日標誌著穆斯林結束一個月的齋戒，慶祝活動包括分享美食、互贈禮物和向貧困人群施捨。

Eid al-Fitr, one of the most significant festivals in Islam, marks the end of the month-long fasting period for Muslims. Celebrations include sharing delicious meals, exchanging gifts, and giving alms to the less fortunate.

7-6-1

2023 年 4 月 23 日，在印度尼西亞沃諾索博，人們參加在開齋節期間舉行的熱氣球節。（新華社稿，阿貢攝）

People prepare to release hot air balloons during a balloon festival on the Eid al-Fitr holiday at Ronggolawe Stadion in Wonosobo, Central Java, Indonesia, on April 23, 2023. (Photo by Agung Supriyanto / Xinhua)

2022 年 5 月 3 日，在印控克什米爾地區冬季首府查謨，人們進行開齋節祈禱。（新華社稿）

People offer Eid al-Fitr prayers in Jammu, the winter capital of Indian-controlled Kashmir, May 3, 2022. (Xinhua)

2023 年 4 月 23 日，在巴基斯坦西北部白沙瓦，一名男子在店內準備傳統甜點，慶祝開齋節假期。（新華社稿，賽義德‧艾哈邁德攝）

A man prepares traditional sweets at a shop during Eid al-Fitr holiday in northwest Pakistan's Peshawar on April 23, 2023. (Photo by Saeed Ahmad / Xinhua)

7-6-4
2022 年 5 月 3 日，孟加拉國達卡的一座清真寺內，人們正在舉行開齋節祈禱。（新華社稿）

Photo taken on May 3, 2022 shows people performing Eid al-Fitr prayers at a masjid in Dhaka, Bangladesh. (Xinhua)

7-7

宰殺牛羊——宰牲節

宰牲節,又稱古爾邦節,是伊斯蘭教的傳統節日之一。
在這一天,穆斯林會宰殺牲畜,並將肉食分發給家人、
朋友和貧困者。

Eid al-Adha is a traditional Islamic festival. On this
day, Muslims slaughter livestock and distribute the
meat to family, friends, and those in need.

7-7-1

2023 年 6 月 29 日,人們在印度新
德里的一個清真寺進行祈禱。(新
華社稿)

People offer Eid Al-Adha prayers at a
grand mosque in New Delhi, India, June
29, 2023. (Xinhua)

7-7-2

2023 年 6 月 26 日，巴基斯坦白沙瓦的牲畜市場，一名商販牽著他的牲畜。（新華社稿）

A trader holds his animal at a livestock market ahead of Eid al-Adha in northwest Pakistan's Peshawar on June 26, 2023. (Xinhua)

7-7-3

2023 年 6 月 29 日，在印度尼西亞日惹，人們扛著用水果、蔬菜等食物堆成的"小山"遊行，並在遊行結束後"爭搶"食物，以此祈求節日祝福。（新華社稿，阿貢·蘇普里揚托攝）

People "scrambling" for food from piles of fruit and vegetables after the Grebeg Besar procession to celebrate Eid al-Adha in Yogyakarta, Indonesia, on June 29, 2023. (Photo by Agung Supriyanto / Xinhua)

7-7-4

2023 年 6 月 25 日，一個男孩在阿富汗首都喀布爾的牲畜市場上看管待售的羊群。宰牲節臨近，喀布爾牲畜市場上的交易繁忙。（新華社稿，查希爾·汗·查希爾攝）

A boy waits to sell his sheep at a livestock market ahead of Eid al-Adha in Kabul, capital of Afghanistan, June 25, 2023. (Photo by Zahir Khan Zahir / Xinhua)

7-8

印度教婦女盛裝祈禱——女人節

提吉節是印度教節日。在節日期間，已婚婦女要齋戒一天為婚姻生活幸福祈禱，未婚女子則祈禱未來找到好的伴侶。

During the celebration of Hindu festival Teej, married women observe a day-long fast to pray for the happiness of their marital life, while unmarried girls pray to find a good life partner in the future.

7-8-1

2023 年 9 月 18 日，在尼泊爾首都加德滿都，婦女們跳起舞蹈，慶祝提吉節。（新華社稿，哈里·馬哈爾詹攝）

Women celebrate the Teej Festival at Pashupatinath Temple in Kathmandu, Nepal, Sept. 18, 2023. (Photo by Hari Maharjan / Xinhua)

7-8-2

2023 年 8 月 14 日，在印度阿姆利則，當地女子身著鮮艷服裝慶祝提吉節。（新華社稿）

Women in traditional Punjabi attire celebrate the Teej Festival in Amritsar district of India's northern Punjab state, Aug. 14, 2023. (Xinhua)

7-9

水燈寄祝福——水燈節

在泰國傳統節日水燈節，民眾前往河流沿岸施放水燈，祈求未
來平安如意。

During Thailand's traditional Loy Krathong Festival, people
released water lanterns for peace and luck.

7-9-1 這是 2021 年 11 月 19 日在泰國曼谷翁昂運河
上拍攝的水燈。（新華社記者，王騰攝）

A water lantern is seen in the Ong Ang Canal
during the Loy Krathong Festival in Bangkok,
Thailand, on Nov. 19, 2021. (Xinhua / Wang Teng)

7-9-2 2022 年 11 月 8 日晚，在文萊斯里巴加灣
市，一名男子在河邊施放水燈。（新華社
稿，傑弗里·黃攝）

A man releases a water lantern in Bandar Seri
Begawan, Brunei, on Nov. 8, 2022. (Photo by
Jeffrey Wong / Xinhua)

7-9-3

2021 年 11 月 19 日，民眾在泰國曼谷翁昂運河邊放水燈。（新華社記者，王騰攝）

People set afloat water lanterns in the Ong Ang Canal during the Loy Krathong Festival in Bangkok, Thailand, on Nov. 19, 2021. (Xinhua / Wang Teng)

7-10

杜爾加女神的祭典 —— 德賽節

德賽節是尼泊爾最大規模和最重要的節日之一，慶祝尼泊爾教和印度教中象徵善的女神杜爾加的勝利。

Dashain is one of Nepal's largest and most significant festivals, celebrating the victory of the goddess Durga, a symbol of goodness, in both Nepalese and Hindu traditions.

 7-10-1

2023 年 10 月 15 日，德賽節的第一天，在尼泊爾加德滿都，一名軍人向空中鳴槍。（新華社稿，蘇拉韋·什雷斯塔攝）

A member of Nepal Army fires into the air on Ghatasthapana, the first day of Dashain festival, in Kathmandu, Nepal, Oct. 15, 2023. (Photo by Sulav Shrestha / Xinhua)

7-10-2

2023 年 10 月 13 日，在尼泊爾拉利特普爾，一名工匠為一尊神靈雕像著色，準備慶祝即將到來的德賽節。（新華社稿，蘇拉韋·什雷斯塔攝）

An artisan colors a statue of a deity in preparation for the upcoming Dashain festival in Lalitpur, Nepal, Oct. 13, 2023. (Photo by Sulav Shrestha / Xinhua)

7-11

光明驅走黑暗——排燈節

排燈節是印度教等教派的傳統節日。人們在這一天點亮彩燈，燃放煙花，象徵著光明戰勝黑暗、善良戰勝邪惡。

Diwali, or the festival of lights, is a traditional festival observed in Hinduism and other religious traditions. On this day, people illuminate colorful lamps and set off fireworks, symbolizing the triumph of light over darkness and goodness over evil.

7-11-1

2023 年 11 月 11 日，在印度博帕爾，女性們點燃煙花慶祝排燈節，也被稱為光明節。（新華社稿）

Women play with firecrackers as they celebrate Diwali festival, also known as festival of lights, in Bhopal, India, Nov. 11, 2023. (Xinhua)

7-11-2

這是 2023 年 11 月 12 日拍攝的排燈節期間的尼泊爾加德滿都夜景。（新華社稿，蘇拉韋·什雷斯塔攝）

This photo taken on Nov. 12, 2023 shows a night view of the Kathmandu Valley during the festival of lights, in Kathmandu, Nepal. (Photo by Sulav Shrestha / Xinhua)

7-12

嘆為觀止 —— 熱氣球節

澳大利亞與新西蘭每年舉辦熱氣球節。人們聚在一起欣賞夢幻般的美景，感受飛行的樂趣。

Annual hot air balloon festivals in Australia and New Zealand gather people to admire the dreamy view of hot air balloons and experience the joy of flying.

7-12-1 & 7-12-2

2023 年 3 月 12 日，在澳大利亞堪培拉，熱氣球飛過伯利‧格里芬湖上空。2023 年堪培拉熱氣球節於 3 月 11 日至 19 日舉行，吸引眾多民眾前來觀賞。（新華社稿，儲晨攝）

A hot air balloon flies over the Lake Burley Griffin during the annual Canberra Balloon Spectacular festival in Canberra, Australia, March 12, 2023. The annual Canberra Balloon Spectacular festival, a hot air balloon festival, is held this year from March 11 to 19. (Photo by Chu Chen / Xinhua)

7-12-3 & 7-12-4

2023 年 3 月 15 日清晨，在新西蘭漢密爾頓，人們聚集在湖邊觀看熱氣球升空。2023 懷卡托熱氣球節於 3 月 14 日至 18 日在新西蘭內陸城鎮漢密爾頓舉行。（新華社記者，郭磊攝）

Hot-air balloons are seen during the 5-day Balloons Over Waikato Festival in Hamilton, New Zealand, March 15, 2023. (Xinhua / Guo Lei)

陸海山川是自然地理，也是人類與其他地球生命的生存環境。除地震、海嘯與火山等特大自然災害之外，氣候變化導致全球變暖，加劇極端天氣，造成如更長的乾旱、更多的降水、更高的氣溫等災害，殃及生態系統、生物多樣性以及人類的居住環境與生活生產活動。"陸海家園"通過展示亞太國家地理環境、自然景色、四季風光與城鄉面貌，揭示氣候變化的影響，並體現生態環境保護的迫切需要。

The land and sea, where mountains and rivers reside, represent not only the natural geography but also the living environment for humans and other Earthly life forms. Apart from major natural disasters like earthquakes, tsunamis, and volcanic eruptions, recent years have seen climate change leading to global warming, exacerbating extreme weather conditions. This has resulted in longer droughts, increased precipitation, higher temperatures, and other disasters, negatively affecting ecosystems, biodiversity, as well as human habitats and livelihoods.

The "Land and Sea Homelands" images, through three thematic units of natural disasters, shared habitats and seasons, as well as countryside and cultural landscapes, showcase the geographical environments, natural scenery, seasonal beauty, and urban-rural landscapes of Asia-Pacific countries. They reveal the impacts of climate change and underscore the urgency of environmental conservation.

8

陸海家園
Land and Sea Homelands

自然災害 Natural Disasters

地震、林火，以及氣候變化帶來的全球變暖和極端天氣加劇，如更長的乾旱、更多的降水、更高的氣溫以及更嚴重的衍生地質災害，影響到生態系統、生物多樣性以及人類的居住環境、日常生活和生產活動。

Earthquakes, wildfires, and climate change-induced global warming and extreme weather events, such as longer droughts, increased precipitation, higher temperatures, and more severe derived geological disasters, impact ecosystems, biodiversity, and human living environments, daily lives, and productive activities.

8-1-1

2020 年 1 月 31 日，澳大利亞首都堪培拉南部受到林火威脅，澳大利亞首都地區進入緊急狀態。（新華社稿，劉暢暢攝）

Photo taken on Jan. 31, 2020 shows a bushfire in the Orroral Valley, south of Canberra, Australia. Authorities have declared a bushfire state of emergency in the Australian Capital Territory (ACT). (Photo by Liu Changchang / Xinhua)

8-1

林火

2019 年 6 月至 2020 年 5 月，高溫天氣和乾旱導致澳大利亞多地共數百場林火肆虐，有 "黑色夏季"（Black Summer）之稱。高峰為 2019 年 12 月到 2020 年 1 月。澳大利亞 6 個州中有 4 個受到影響，其中東海岸的新南威爾士州和維多利亞州是重災區。

2020 年 8 月發佈的有關初步報告顯示：林火直接致死至少 33 人，煙霾導致多人死亡並給一些民眾造成嚴重心理創傷；大約 30 億隻動物或被燒死，或無處棲息，一些珍稀物種損失嚴重；3,000 多所房屋燒毀；過火面積為大約 2,400 萬公頃到 4,000 萬公頃；預計給農林業、旅遊業等領域造成 36 億澳元經濟損失。有學者說，山林大火一定程度上受到氣候變化的影響。

2020 年 1 月澳大利亞首都堪培拉因林火近 20 年來首次宣佈進入緊急狀態。西南方向約 40 公里的納馬吉國家公園佔地 10 多萬公頃，約佔堪培拉地區面積的 45%，是當地重要生態保護區。在 2020 年 1 月林火中，公園過火面積約 8.6 萬公頃，超過總面積的 80%。

From June 2019 to May 2020, high temperatures and drought conditions contributed to hundreds of across Australia, an event widely known as the Black Summer. The peak of the crisis occurred between December 2019 and January 2020. Four of Australia's six states were affected, with New South Wales and Victoria on the east coast being the hardest hit.

In August 2020, a sobering report unveiled the devastating toll of wildfires in Australia. The direct loss of life reached at least 33, while the insidious smoke claimed additional lives and inflicted profound psychological trauma on countless others. An estimated 3 billion animals perished in the flames or were left homeless, with endangered species facing particularly devastating losses. Over 3,000 homes were reduced to ashes, and the inferno engulfed an area between 24 million and 40 million hectares. The economic ramifications loomed large, with anticipated losses of a staggering 3.6 billion Australian dollars across agriculture, forestry, and tourism. Scholars emphasized the undeniable influence of climate change in exacerbating these catastrophic wildfires.

Meanwhile, in January 2020, Canberra, Australia's capital, declared a state of emergency due to wildfires for the first time in nearly two decades. The Namadgi National Park, located approximately 40 km southwest of the city, encompasses over 100,000 hectares—constituting nearly 45 percent of the Canberra region and serving as a vital ecological sanctuary. However, in the wildfires of January 2020, a staggering 86,000 hectares of the park were engulfed, representing over 80 percent of its total area.

8-1-2

這是 2020 年 1 月 18 日在澳大利亞莫戈鎮拍攝的被林火燒毀的車輛。（新華社稿，儲晨攝）

Photo taken on Jan. 18, 2020 shows the car destroyed by the bushfire in the town of Mogo, a two-hour drive from Canberra, Australia. At least 28 people have lost their lives and more than 2,000 homes been destroyed across the country in this bushfire season in Australia. (Photo by Chu Chen / Xinhua)

8-1-3

這是 2020 年 1 月 18 日距澳大利亞首都堪培拉約一個小時車程的林火過火區域。至少 28 人在火災中喪生，全國 2,000 多所房屋被毀。（新華社稿，儲晨攝）

Photo taken on Jan. 18, 2020 shows a bushfire area, about a one-hour drive from Canberra, Australia. At least 28 people have lost their lives and more than 2,000 homes been destroyed across the country in this bushfire season in Australia. (Photo by Chu Chen / Xinhua)

8-1-4

2020 年 1 月 5 日，在新西蘭奧克蘭，汽車行駛在高速公路上。

澳大利亞東南海岸森林大火產生的煙塵當日飄過塔斯曼海，抵達新西蘭北島北部地
區上空，新西蘭最大城市奧克蘭籠罩在黃褐色煙塵中。（新華社稿，李橋橋攝）

A local highway is pictured against an orange-colored sky as smoke generated by Australian
bushfires hit Auckland, New Zealand, Jan. 5, 2020. (Photo by Li Qiaoqiao / Xinhua)

8-2

地震

部分東南亞、南亞與南太平洋島嶼國家如菲律賓、印度尼西亞、尼泊爾、阿富汗、湯加等地，以及日本，處於 Ring of Fire 環太平洋地震帶或火環帶，或從印度尼西亞爪哇島、蘇門打臘島延伸至喜馬拉雅山脈、地中海以及大西洋的阿爾卑斯帶上，板塊移動劇烈，地震、強震、海嘯與火山爆發等災害頻發，導致生命與經濟損失，以及次生與衍生災害。

In regions of South Asia, Southeast Asia, and South Pacific island countries, including the Philippines, Indonesia, Nepal, Afghanistan and Tonga, as well as Japan, a significant portion of the countries lie within the notorious "Ring of Fire", also known as the Circum-Pacific Belt. This volatile zone stretches from Java and Sumatra in Indonesia, extending to the Himalayas, the Mediterranean, and the Alpine belts of the Atlantic. Characterized by intense tectonic plate movements, this region frequently experiences a slew of natural disasters, including earthquakes, powerful tremors, tsunamis, and volcanic eruptions. These catastrophic events result in loss of life and economic devastation, as well as secondary and derivative calamities.

8-2-1

尼泊爾西部扎澤爾果德和魯古姆西區兩縣 2023 年 11 月 3 日午夜發生 6.4 級地震。據官方消息，截至當地時間 11 月 6 日 19 時，3 日地震已造成 157 人死亡、349 人受傷，另有 3.5 萬多所房屋受損或完全倒塌。這是 2023 年 11 月 6 日在尼泊爾西部扎澤爾果德地震災區拍攝的一人走過建築物廢墟的照片。（新華社稿，蘇拉韋·什雷斯塔攝）

In the early hours of Nov. 3, 2023, a powerful earthquake measuring 6.4 on the Richter scale struck the districts of Jajarkot and Rukum West in western Nepal. As of 7:00 PM local time on Nov. 6, the quake has tragically claimed the lives of 157 individuals and left 349 others injured, according to official reports. More than 35,000 homes were either damaged or completely destroyed in the disaster. In this photo, a man walks past a house destroyed in an earthquake in Jajarkot, Nepal, on Nov. 6, 2023. (Photo by Sulav Shrestha / Xinhua)

8-2-2

這是 2022 年 6 月 23 日在阿富汗東部帕克提卡省拍攝的地
震倖存當地兒童。（新華社稿，塞夫拉赫曼・薩菲攝）

Photo taken on June 23, 2022 shows survivors from an earthquake
in Paktika province, Afghanistan. (Photo by Saifurahman Safi /
Xinhua)

8-3

火山噴發

湯加位於環太平洋火山地震帶，洪阿哈阿帕伊島是高度活躍的湯加─克馬德克群島火山弧的一部分，位於首都努庫阿洛法以北約 65 公里處。2022 年 1 月 14 日，洪阿哈阿帕伊島海底火山噴發，大量火山灰、氣體與水蒸氣形成巨大雲團；15 日第二次劇烈噴發，火山灰柱直徑達約 5 千米、高 20 千米。觀測發現努庫阿洛法附近有 1.2 米高的海嘯，主要街道和不少建築被海水淹沒。火山灰遍覆努庫阿洛法。當地通信網絡受到嚴重干擾。

Tonga, situated within the volatile Circum-Pacific seismic belt, is home to the highly active Tonga-Kermadec island arc-Hunga Ha'apai island, located approximately 65 km north of the capital, Nuku'alofa. On Jan. 14, 2022, an underwater volcano near Hunga Ha'apai erupted spectacularly, spewing vast clouds of volcanic ash, gases, and steam into the atmosphere.

The following day witnessed a second intense eruption, with a volcanic ash column reaching a diameter of approximately 5 km and soaring to a height of 20 km. Observations revealed a tsunami measuring 1.2 meters near Nuku'alofa, inundating major thoroughfares and numerous buildings with seawater. The city was blanketed in volcanic ash, and local communication networks suffered severe disruptions in the aftermath of the cataclysmic events.

8-3-1

南太平洋島國湯加的洪阿哈阿帕伊島 2022 年 1 月 14 日和 15 日發生火山噴發，首都努庫阿洛法觀測到海嘯。這是 2022 年 1 月 20 日早晨在湯加首都努庫阿洛法拍攝的遭受海嘯侵襲後的街道和房屋。（新華社稿，馬里安攝）

Photo taken on Jan. 20, 2022 shows houses and infrastructures hit by tsunami in Nuku'alofa, capital of Tonga. On Friday and Saturday, the Hunga Tonga-Hunga Ha'apai volcano in Tonga erupted violently and triggered tsunami in Tonga. (Photo by Marian Kupu / Xinhua)

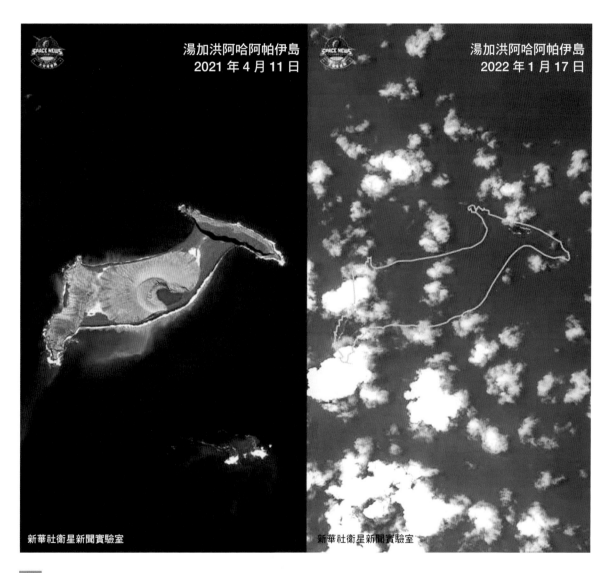

8-3-2

這是 2021 年 4 月 11 日太平洋島國湯加洪阿哈阿帕伊島的衛星雲圖（左圖）和 2022 年 1 月 17 日的衛星雲圖（右圖）。右圖上基於地質坐標繪製的橙色曲綫顯示了洪加哈阿帕伊島在海底火山噴發前的輪廓。2022 年 1 月 14 日至 15 日，洪加哈阿帕伊島海底火山爆發，引發了一場海嘯。（新華社稿，新華社衛星新聞實驗室供圖）

The combined satellite images show Tonga's Hunga Ha'apai island on April 11, 2021 (L) and Jan. 17, 2022. The orange curve on the right picture, drawn based on geological coordinates, shows the outline of Tonga's Hunga Ha'apai island before the underwater volcano eruption. The Hunga Tonga-Hunga Ha'apai underwater volcano of the Pacific island nation of Tonga erupted on Jan. 14-15, 2022 and triggered a tsunami. (Xinhua's Space News Lab / Handout via Xinhua)

8-3-3

這是 2023 年 3 月 11 日在印度尼西亞日惹拍攝的噴發的默拉皮火山。默拉皮火山是印尼最活躍的活火山之一。（新華社稿，阿貢・蘇普里揚托攝）

Volcanic materials spew out from Mount Merapi in Yogyakarta, Indonesia, March 11, 2023. Mount Merapi is one of Indonesia's most active volcanos. (Photo by Agung Supriyanto / Xinhua)

8-3-4

塔阿爾火山 2020 年 1 月 12 日下午開始劇烈活動並噴出大量火山灰。據菲國家減災管理委員會，離火山最近的 3 個鎮約 1 萬名居民疏散。這是 2020 年 1 月 13 日，在菲律賓八打雁省塔阿爾火山附近，一隻牛身上覆蓋著火山灰和泥漿的照片。（新華社稿，烏馬利攝）

An ash-covered cow is seen as Taal volcano erupts in Batangas Province, the Philippines, Jan. 13, 2020. (Photo by Rouelle Umali / Xinhua)

8-4

海嘯

2011 年 3 月 11 日，日本東北發生 9.0 級地震並繼發海嘯，福島第一核電站 1 至 4 號機組發生嚴重核泄漏事故，其中 1 至 3 號機組堆芯熔毀。此後因用水冷卻熔毀堆芯以及雨水和地下水等流過，每天產生大量高濃度核污染水。2021 年，日本政府與東京電力公司決定向太平洋排放核污染水。2023 年 8 月 24 日開始實施第一輪排放。福島第一核電站排放前儲存的核污染水超過 130 萬噸。日本核污染水排海引起本國民眾、鄰國與南太平洋島國等國政府與民眾強烈抗議。

On March 11, 2011, a devastating 9.0-magnitude earthquake struck northeastern Japan, triggering a subsequent tsunami. The Fukushima Daiichi nuclear power plant experienced a catastrophic nuclear meltdown, with reactors 1 through 3 suffering core meltdowns. In the aftermath, vast quantities of highly contaminated water have been generated daily due to the necessity of cooling the molten reactor cores, as well as rainwater and groundwater seepage.

In 2021, the Japanese government, in collaboration with Tokyo Electric Power Company (TEPCO), made a controversial decision to discharge the nuclear-contaminated water into the Pacific Ocean. The first round of this contentious discharge began on Aug. 24, 2023, with over 1.3 million tons of stored contaminated water from the Fukushima Daiichi nuclear power plant being released. The decision has sparked strong protests from its own citizens in Japan, neighboring countries, and South Pacific island nations.

8-4-1

2021 年 4 月 13 日，抗議者在日本東京的首相官邸外反對福島核污水排入大海。

無視國內國際輿論的質疑和反對，日本政府 13 日召開有關內閣會議正式決定將福島第一核電站上百萬噸核污水經過濾並稀釋後排入大海，排放將於約 2 年後開始。（新華社記者，杜瀟逸攝）

People rally to protest against the Japanese government's decision to discharge contaminated radioactive wastewater in Fukushima Prefecture into the sea, in Tokyo, capital of Japan, April 13, 2021.

Japanese government on the day decided to discharge contaminated radioactive wastewater in Fukushima Prefecture into the sea amid domestic and international opposition. (Xinhua / Du Xiaoyi)

8-4-2

2023 年 8 月 14 日，懸掛橫幅標語的漁船在韓國仁川沿岸碼頭海域進行海上遊行，抗議日本核污染水排海。（新華社記者，王益亮攝）

Fishing boats sail to protest against Japan's planned discharge of radioactive wastewater into the ocean, in waters off Incheon, South Korea, Aug. 14, 2023.

Over 50 fishing vessels set out from a pier in Incheon on a parallel voyage, sailing around for about one and a half hours with banners attached on the vessels that read "Use the Fukushima contaminated wastewater as drinking water in Japan," and "The ocean is not a dumpster for the Fukushima nuclear-contaminated wastewater." (Xinhua / Wang Yiliang)

8-5

海平面上升

8-5

這是 2023 年 6 月 8 日在印度尼西亞中爪哇省淡目角廷布爾斯洛科村拍攝的被海水包圍的住宅區。海平面上升與地表沉降導致該地區一些村落被海水包圍。（新華社稿，阿迪蒂亞・亨德拉攝）

This aerial photo taken on June 8, 2023 shows a residential area surrounded by water at Timbulsloko village in Demak, Central Java, Indonesia. Rising sea levels and subsidence of the land surface have resulted in some villages surrounded by sea water. (Photo by Aditya Irawan / Xinhua)

8-6

洪水

8-6

這是 2021 年 9 月 6 日在孟加拉國博格拉拍攝的被洪水包圍的房屋（航拍照片）。受季風雨季影響，孟加拉國博格拉地區遭遇洪澇災害。（新華社稿，薩利姆攝）

Aerial photo shows flood-affected houses in Bogura, some 197 km northwest of Dhaka, Bangladesh on Sept. 6, 2021. Heavy monsoon rains have triggered severe flooding in the Bogura district of Bangladesh, leaving thousands of people affected and disrupting daily life. (Photo by Salim / Xinhua)

8-7

颶風、颱風

2023 年 2 月 16 日，新西蘭國防軍在新西蘭北島東部災區開展救援工作。新西蘭政府 18 日表示，颶風 "加布麗埃爾" 導致北島東部大量道路橋樑損毀，該地區仍有數千人因通訊中斷失聯。（新華社稿，新西蘭國防部供圖）

Rescuers work on cyclone-affected North Island in New Zealand on Feb. 16, 2023. The New Zealand government announced on Feb. 18 that Hurricane "Gabrielle" has caused extensive damage to roads and bridges in the eastern part of the North Island. As a result of communication disruptions, several thousand people in the affected area remain unaccounted for and unreachable. (NZDF / Handout via Xinhua)

2023 年 1 月，新西蘭最大城市奧克蘭遭遇強降雨所致洪災；2 月，颶風 "加布麗埃爾" 襲擊奧克蘭所處的新西蘭北島，引發洪水、山體滑坡等，造成 11 人死亡以及巨大損失。〔據新西蘭政府估算，兩場災害所致損失可能高達 145 億新西蘭元（90 億美元），為 2011 年第二大城市克賴斯特徹奇大地震以來最為嚴重的自然災害損失。〕"加布麗埃爾" 颶風迫使新西蘭宣佈進入國家緊急狀態，這是其歷史上的第三次，之前兩次因 2011 年第二大城市克賴斯特徹奇大地震和 2020 年新冠疫情暴發。

In January 2023, New Zealand's largest city, Auckland, experienced severe flooding due to heavy rainfall. In February, Cyclone Gabrielle struck the North Island, where Auckland is located, causing widespread flooding, landslides, and significant damage. The cyclone resulted in 11 fatalities and extensive destruction. The New Zealand government estimates that the two disasters could cost up to 14.5 billion New Zealand dollars (9 billion U.S. dollars), making it the country's most costly natural disaster since the 2011 Christchurch earthquake. Cyclone Gabrielle prompted New Zealand to declare a national state of emergency, only the third in its history, with the previous two being the 2011 Christchurch earthquake and the 2020 COVID-19 outbreak.

這是 2020 年 11 月 16 日在菲律賓黎剎省拍攝的颱風 "環高" 過境受災區域。（新華社稿，烏馬利攝）

Photo taken on Nov. 16, 2020 shows damaged residences in the wake of Typhoon Vamco in Rizal Province, the Philippines. (Photo by Rouelle Umali / Xinhua)

8-8

乾旱

8-8

這是 2023 年 10 月 6 日在印度尼西亞中爪哇省沃諾吉里拍攝的旱季乾涸見底的水庫。據印尼氣象部門，受厄爾尼諾現象影響，2023 年印度尼西亞旱災更加嚴重。（新華社稿，澤洛攝）

Wooden boats are seen on the dried-up bed during dry season at Gajah Mungkur reservoir in Wonogiri, Central Java, Indonesia, on Oct. 6, 2023. According to Indonesia's meteorological department, the drought disaster in Indonesia was exacerbated in 2023 due to the influence of the El Niño phenomenon. (Photo by Bram Selo / Xinhua)

8-9

蝗災

8-9

2020 年，繼 2 月沙漠蝗自非洲跨境而來侵襲印度之後，5 月上旬以來印度再次遭遇蝗災，多地出現大量蝗蟲並造成農田損毀，部分城市區域也出現蝗蟲群。印度政府說，這是印度近 30 年來遭受的最嚴重蝗災。

2020 年 5 月 25 日，在印度拉賈斯坦邦首府齋浦爾，大批蝗蟲徘徊在當地住宅區。（新華社稿）

After battling a devastating desert locust invasion from Africa in February, India is facing another wave of the ravenous pests since early May 2020. Swarms of locusts have descended upon multiple regions, causing widespread crop damage and even appearing in some urban areas. The Indian government has called it the worst locust outbreak in nearly 30 years.

Photo taken on May 25, 2020 shows swarms of locusts in the residential areas of Jaipur, the capital city of India's western state of Rajasthan. (Xinhua)

共同家園 Our Homeland

自然環境是人類和其他地球生命的共同家園。保護環境與生物多樣性至關重要。

The natural environment serves as the shared habitat for humanity and all other life forms on Earth. Preserving the environment and biodiversity is of paramount importance.

8-10

動植物

8-10-1

2022 年 3 月 30 日，在新西蘭南島福克斯西海岸溫帶雨林中，一簇蜜環菌在暗夜中播撒孢子。（新華社稿，楊柳攝）

Photo shows the Armillaria novae-zelandiae in a temperate rainforest on the South Island of New Zealand, March 30, 2022. Armillaria novae-zelandiae is one of three Armillaria species that have been identified in New Zealand, also nick-named Honey mushroom. It grows most abundantly from March to May in wet forests primarily. (Photo by Yang Liu / Xinhua)

8-10-2

這是 2022 年 4 月 20 日在馬來亞柔佛州拍攝的凱木迪（音譯）河沿岸紅樹林。（新華社記者，朱煒攝）

The mangrove swamp is pictured along the Kemudi river in Johor state, Malaysia, April 20, 2022. (Xinhua / Zhu Wei)

8-10-3

小藍企鵝是新西蘭分佈地域最廣、數量最多的一種。小藍企鵝是企鵝家族中身材最嬌小的品種，成年小藍企鵝身長約 25—35 公分，體重在 1—1.5 公斤。小藍企鵝生性膽小，總藏身於人跡罕至處。每年 4 月 25 日是世界企鵝日。(新華社記者，郭磊攝)

Little Blue Penguins are seen at a natural reserve in Dunedin, South Island of New Zealand, April 22, 2021. After a day of fishing, little blue penguins came ashore and returned home to their nests under the cover of darkness in Dunedin. The Little Blue Penguin is the most widespread and populous species in New Zealand. As the smallest member of the penguin family, adult Little Blue Penguins typically measure about 25-35 centimeters in length and weigh between 1-1.5 kilograms. These penguins are inherently timid and often seek refuge in remote areas away from human activity. Every year, April 25th is observed as World Penguin Day. (Xinhua / Guo Lei)

8-10-4

這是 2023 年 10 月 16 日在緬甸首都內比都野生動物
園拍攝的犀牛。〔新華社稿，苗覺梭（音譯）攝〕

Rhinos are seen at the Safari park in Nay Pyi Taw, Myanmar,
Oct. 16, 2023. (Photo by Myo Kyaw Soe / Xinhua)

8-10-5

這是 2021 年 8 月 12 日在澳大利亞堪培拉馬利根平原自然保護區拍攝的袋鼠。馬利根平原自然保護區位於澳大利亞首都地區東北邊緣，佔地約 750 公頃。（新華社稿，劉暢暢攝）

Photo taken on Aug. 12, 2021 shows a kangaroo in the Mulligans Flat Nature Reserve in Canberra, Australia. The Mulligans Flat Nature Reserve, located on the northeastern border of the Australian Capital Territory (ACT), covers approximately 750 hectares of land. (Photo by Liu Changchang / Xinhua)

8-11

家園

8-11-1

2022 年 2 月 10 日，一名男子在日本東京淺草寺拍照。（新華社記者，張笑宇攝）

A man takes photos at Asakusa's Sensoji Temple in Tokyo, Japan, Feb. 10, 2022. (Xinhua / Zhang Xiaoyu)

8-11-2

這是 2021 年 10 月 24 日在孟加拉
國蘇納姆甘傑一條河流上拍攝的採
砂的船隻。(新華社稿,薩利姆攝)

Aerial photo taken on Oct. 24, 2021
shows a view of a quarry in the Jadukata
river in Sunamganj, Bangladesh. (Photo
by Salim / Xinhua)

8-11-3
2023 年 1 月 1 日，人們在新加坡濱海灣觀賞新年煙花與無人機燈光秀表演，辭舊迎新。（新華社稿，鄧智煒攝）
Tourists view the Marina Bay Countdown 2023 fireworks and drone light show from Marina Bay Sands Sky Park Observation Deck, in Singapore on Jan. 1, 2023. (Photo by Then Chih Wey / Xinhua)

8-11-4

2023 年 10 月 22 日，遊客在泰國大城阿瑜陀耶古城遺址遊覽。
位於泰國中部的大城府約建於 1350 年，是泰國著名古都。
1991 年，大城府阿瑜陀耶古城被聯合國教科文組織列為世界
遺產，保護面積 289 公頃。(新華社稿，拉亨攝)

A tourist is seen at the Ayutthaya Historical Park in Ayutthaya,
Thailand, Oct. 22, 2023. Located in central Thailand, Ayutthaya was
built around 1350 and is the famous ancient capital of Thailand. In
1991, the ancient city of Ayutthaya was listed as a UNESCO World
Heritage Site with a protected area of 289 hectares. (Photo by Rachen
Sageamsak / Xinhua)

8-11-5

這是 2023 年 12 月 24 日拍攝的圖片，
美軍轟炸將阿富汗東部瓦爾達克省一個
村莊夷為廢墟。（新華社稿，塞夫拉赫
曼・薩菲攝）

This photo taken on Dec. 24, 2023 shows
houses destroyed by bombardments
conducted by the U.S. troops in Ismael Khil
village of Wardak Province, Afghanistan.
(Photo by Saifurahman Safi / Xinhua)

8-11-6
這是 2023 年 11 月 4 日拍攝的航拍圖片，顯示了老撾萬象的農民正在麥田裏辛勤勞作，老撾此時已經迎來了又一個豐收季節。（新華社稿，凱伊凱歐·賽亞塞恩攝）

This aerial photo taken on Nov. 4, 2023 shows farmers working in a grain field in Vientiane, Laos. Laos has ushered in the harvest season. (Photo by Kaikeo Saiyasane / Xinhua)

疫情生活 Battle Against COVID-19 Pandemic

2020 年新冠疫情開始衝擊全球，成為一大公共衛生緊急事件，一度嚴重影響了人們的生活和生產活動。人們以樂觀的精神在抗擊疫情中"非常態"生活。

In 2020, the COVID-19 pandemic swept across the globe, evolving into a significant public health crisis that profoundly disrupted daily life and economic activities. Yet, amidst these challenges, people persevered with resilience, navigating through this unprecedented "New Normal" era with an unwavering spirit of optimism.

8-12

生活

8-12-1

2020 年 5 月 1 日，在尼泊爾首都加德滿都一場婚禮上，佩戴口罩的新人相互表達愛意。（新華社稿，蘇拉韋·什雷斯塔攝）

A bride and her groom wear face masks at their wedding ceremony in Kathmandu, Nepal, on May 1, 2020. (Photo by Sulav Shrestha / Xinhua)

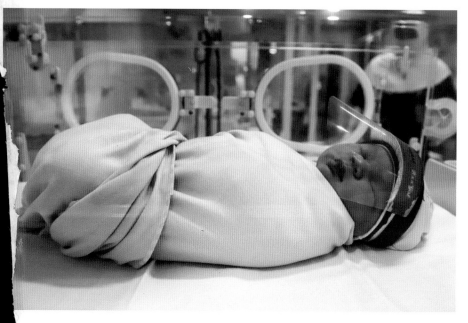

2020 年 4 月 17 日，在印度尼西亞雅加達，一名剛出生的嬰兒佩戴著防護面罩。（新華社稿）

An Indonesian new born baby wears a face shield as a protection against COVID-19 at Tambak Maternity Hospital in Jakarta, Indonesia, April 17, 2020. (Xinhua)

2021 年 4 月 26 日，在印度首都新德里，人們在一家商店門前排隊為 COVID-19 患者的醫用氧氣瓶充氣。（新華社稿，帕塔·沙卡爾攝）

People wait in line to refill empty medical oxygen cylinders for COVID-19 patients in front of a shop in New Delhi, India, April 26, 2021. (Photo by Partha Sarkar / Xinhua)

責任編輯　　王　穎

書籍設計　　a_kun

書籍排版　　何秋雲

書　　名　　**亞洲相冊**
　　　　　　Asia Album

著　　者　　《亞洲相冊》編委會

出　　版　　三聯書店（香港）有限公司
　　　　　　香港北角英皇道 499 號北角工業大廈 20 樓
　　　　　　Joint Publishing (H.K.) Co., Ltd.
　　　　　　20/F., North Point Industrial Building,
　　　　　　499 King's Road, North Point, Hong Kong

香港發行　　香港聯合書刊物流有限公司
　　　　　　香港新界荃灣德士古道 220-248 號 16 樓

印　　刷　　美雅印刷製本有限公司
　　　　　　香港九龍觀塘榮業街 6 號 4 樓 A 室

版　　次　　2024 年 7 月香港第 1 版第 1 次印刷

規　　格　　16 開（185 mm × 245 mm）224 面

國際書號　　ISBN　978-962-04-5463-9